Praise for 1

"Have you ever asked yourself, 'Why me?' If so, this heartfelt book will draw you in as you learn about God's gracious and deep love for you. Julie LaQuey beautifully explores this as she shares her experiences of having a daughter with unique needs. You will walk alongside her family as God works in and through them to teach His truths, demonstrate His love, and shine His light to others. She brings hope to families experiencing unique situations to change the question of lament to, 'Why *not* me?' In reading this book, I was deeply reminded that we are all beautifully and uniquely created because we are loved by God and He works through *all* of our experiences for His glory!"

Sherri Seligson, M.Ed.
Author, Speaker, Scientist

"The stories that Julie shares of God's faithfulness through the joys and the sorrows, the beauty and the brokenness, will both encourage and challenge the reader. Encourage them to pay attention to those around them who are different. Challenge them to have eyes to see God at work in their own lives."

Sarah Stonestreet
Co-Host of The Strong Women Podcast
with The Colson Center for Christian Worldview

"As a pro-life apologist, I am grateful for Julie's story because it is a shining example that defies the current cultural narrative of the value of human life. As a mom, I am simultaneously challenged and deeply inspired. This is a book for every parent! It is a touching tribute not only to Abby and the radiant light that she is, but to Tyce, Caleb, Luke, and — at the core — to God who sees, loves, guides and blesses. Julie's stunning transparency is interwoven with practical lessons and advice, stories that will make you marvel, a beautiful faith that just can't help but shimmer through her words, and strength that is rooted in humble submission. Be ready to remember the foundational truth that Abby LaQuey has known all along — you are loved."

Megan Almon
Speaker with Life Training Institute
Faculty Member at Summit Ministries

"As a Mom of a daughter with unique needs, I found *Powered by Love* encouraging, hopeful, and full of wisdom. The beautiful story of Abby is interwoven throughout the book with practical guidance about navigating diagnoses, educational decisions, therapies, friendships, finances, and faith. Julie is a Mom who has 'been there - done that,' and I am thankful for the insights she shares."

Bri Heflin
Mom of 4

"I am a mom of three young children, a daughter who is three and two boys ages two and one.

"We are in the process of adopting our middle son who has quite a list of unique needs. Needless to say, it has been a very busy time of learning and growing as we begin to parent these three beautiful, opinionated, and sometimes exhausting little blessings. There are often times that bring doubt and make both me and my husband wonder about how well we are doing as parents. *Powered by Love* has been a wonderful read and a blessing to me as a new mom of a child with unique needs. It allows readers to feel like they are talking and engaged with a mentoring mama who has already walked the path ahead. The book brings readers first and foremost back to Scripture to put our parenting and advocating into clear biblical perspective.

"Along with being a mother to my three children, I am also a pediatric physical therapist and enjoy learning from all of my patients and families as I try to walk alongside them in their various stages of life. Reading *Powered by Love* also impacted my working routines as it brings to light ways that therapists and caregivers can choose to be a light and an encouragement to families through looking at a child's many strengths rather than only analyzing their weaknesses."

Katelynn Bolt
Mom of 3 and
Pediatric Physical Therapist

"As a pastor to young families, I am ecstatic to see that Julie's family has shared the most intimate parts of what we as a church get to see lived out in their lives in real time. They've embraced the call that God has placed on their lives and seen God faithfully provide time and time again. This book will both challenge and encourage you to see the adventure that awaits you in parenting God's greatest blessing--your kids!"

Andy Bowen
Associate Life Stage Pastor
Christ Chapel Bible Church

"*Powered by Love* is a beautiful story of encouragement and hope. The LaQueys' story had a calming effect on us as parents still new to this journey where fears of the unknown can sometimes creep in. The ways in which they intentionally sought to learn from their daughter and the beauty she brings to their family and those around them are very inspiring."

Randy & Jennifer DeLaCruz
Parents of 4-year-old Abigail who has Down syndrome

Powered by Love

Wisdom and Hope for Families with Unique Needs

Julie LaQuey

Powered by Love: Wisdom and Hope for Families with Unique Needs

© Copyright 2022 by Julie LaQuey

Edited by Elizabeth Newenhuyse

Published by Writing Momentum LLC

Cover design, print and ebook formatting by Writing Momentum LLC

Dedicated to my daughter Abby, who I am certain makes the Father rejoice, along with her brothers, Caleb and Luke, all of whom have saved me from my own selfishness and filled my life with joy beyond anything I could have imagined.

1 Timothy 2:15; Ephesians 3:14-21

Contents

Foreword

Have you heard about the parents who had a second child because their first was easy to raise? Tyce and Julie LaQuey chose to have a second for a different reason. They enjoyed parenting their son, Caleb, and wanted him to have a sibling. Julie always wanted many children.

Their daughter, Abby, was born with Down syndrome. Neither Julie nor Tyce thought parenting her would be easy, but it wasn't hard for them. They did what any good parent does. They found out what they needed to know and then did what they needed to do.

Well, it wasn't as easy as that one sentence makes it seem—or Julie wouldn't have had enough material to write a book. What made it easy? In these pages you'll read about the depth of their love for God and each other and how God's love for them changed them. You'll learn about how they grew and what they learned that caused them to adopt new, wise perspectives and healthy expectations. These adjustments resulted in beliefs, attitudes, decisions, and actions that made raising Abby easy.

I've known Abby almost her entire life. I met her and the whole family when she was a few years old and needed prayer for a medical challenge. We've all been friends through church, and I've always respected and enjoyed Julie. I was thrilled when she began thinking about this book because she's an excellent writer and has many stories and truths worthy of sharing.

Recommending this book to you is easy. I'm confident God will use all He taught Tyce, Julie, and Abby to equip, empower, and strengthen you. Get ready!

Kathy Koch, PhD
Founder of Celebrate Kids
& Ignite the Family

Prologue: First Things First, Last Things First

My daughter Abby has Down syndrome. In a time when others like her are often aborted, Abby has demonstrated confidence, even as a young child, knowing that she is valued and loved. As her mother, I recognize it is not my love for her that has given her this confidence, nor is it her father's love that has provided her with this confidence. Certainly, my husband Tyce and I contributed something to her understanding, but ultimately, her source of confidence is not from us.

This book details many of the ways God has demonstrated His love towards our family and towards Abby in particular. Through reading about our experiences, you may begin to have a better understanding and recognition of how much God loves you also. As a result, you will inevitably be empowered by this love in your relationships. It is only as we discover how God loves us that we are able to truly comprehend how to love others.

When we possess an unwavering confidence that we are loved, we then also possess the freedom to express love and joy to others. This freedom is a common characteristic that I have found among many families with unique needs. Years ago, I began to help advocate for friends in our local public schools, and I established a group called Families with Unique Needs (F.U.N.). Establishing this group was my attempt to include others in my own learning process, to share the information I was learning as soon as I found it. I purposely chose the acronym F.U.N. because I had already begun to see that these families possessed a great love for life and a unique joy that stemmed from their choices and experiences. As our family began to engage with these other families, we saw that they exhibited freedom and joy that clearly came from being different and knowing they are loved just the way they are. We found that as we began to remove pretense and accept and tolerate each other, we also found joy in how we are different. As we opened up to embrace unique ways of thinking, we found many things to laugh about! There is humor in being different, in thinking in different ways, in exploring new perspectives. In the midst of difficulties and challenges, humor can help minimize our trials, magnify our joys, and enhance our celebrations when we overcome.

However, life is not all about fun, and not everything about having Down syndrome is fun. Many of our experiences recorded here begin with significant difficulties or struggles. But they always end with life and joy and beauty. We found that we can have joy even in the midst of difficulty. Every story I've written with the hope that you will be encouraged and renewed and enlightened through reading it, that you also will develop a greater confidence that you are loved, and that you will know the freedom and joy that results from that confidence.

I understand that many who begin to read this book won't read every word, and I want to express grace to those who skip over parts that they feel may not apply to their situation. Our family's experiences have helped us learn and grow, and you can learn and grow from reading about them.

Though you may have the best intentions of finishing a book, you may get distracted by the many other things that demand your time. One section here I don't want you to miss. If you do skip some sections or decide to read the end of the book first, please be sure to read the section titled "The End of the Matter, When All Has Been Heard." It's my prayer that you will discover the main purpose for writing this book and also discover the purpose for our lives here on earth, if you have not already.

Though many of the circumstances we've encountered have been sobering and somber, the joy that results is real and lasting. We have come to recognize that it is through the hardships and difficulties God placed in our lives that He demonstrated His love towards us and led us to experience greater joy. I pray you also will recognize how your joy can be magnified through the hardships of life, that you will possess the freedom that comes as a result of knowing assuredly that you are deeply loved by God, and that you will be empowered to love God and love others well!

An Introduction to Abby

She was five years old and scheduled to have open-heart surgery the following week. She was excited to get dressed up for church that Sunday, and I almost couldn't take my eyes off her soft blonde curls. Her sweet personality and kind heart were evident to everyone who knew her. She possessed a remarkable ability to perceive the feelings of those around her, and somehow, she knew just how to make you feel better when you were hurting. She was tender and delicate and seemed so fragile, but at the same time, she exhibited a strength that could not be denied. She could be stubborn when she knew what she wanted or needed or what someone else needed. Abby had captured our hearts and brought joy that filled our home.

My husband, Tyce, and I recognized the risks that were involved in the surgery. Abby's big brother Caleb, our oldest child, at only seven years old, was much less aware of what was happening but yet had an understanding of the gravity of the situation. He had attended the appointments with us and watched the echocardiogram as it showed blood flowing the wrong direction in her heart. He heard the conversations and prayed with us for her healing.

As our family prepared for Abby's upcoming heart surgery,

many questions still permeated my mind. But there was also peace. We had asked everything we knew to ask. Was this the best time to do the surgery? Was the surgeon experienced in this procedure? We had asked for prayers from everyone we knew, and many people were praying with us. We knew God held her life in His hands. He held our whole family and our future in His hands.

We believed the surgery would be successful and was necessary. But the possibility of complications loomed, and I had to prepare myself for that potential reality. I wanted to hold onto every moment I had with Abby and create as many memories as possible in the time that remained before the procedure. I took pictures; I cemented her sweet little handprint; I took time for extra snuggles and cuddles at every opportunity.

There didn't seem to be enough opportunities. The days were zooming by. Abby's baby brother, Luke, was only two weeks old and required so much of my time and attention. Her older brother, Caleb, needed my attention too, and I already felt guilty that his schoolwork had been pushed aside as we had attended many medical appointments and endured months of me being on bedrest. Everything that was not essential was pushed off until later. Baby shower gifts were still stacked up beside our bed.

It had been a very eventful year. The previous summer, we had decided to begin homeschooling and, at the same time, decided to expand our family. We knew it wouldn't be easy, and I had accepted the fact that my life would be focused on providing for the needs of our children. But I hadn't known at the time that open-heart surgery would be part of our plan for the year. Still, God was providing and meeting all our needs. I simply needed to work to the best of my ability and trust God to take care of everything else. I see now all the amazing ways He did. Many prayers helped us stay calm in the midst of what could have been chaos. It was God that helped us not just survive but thrive to such an extent that we all have very fond memories of those days. We remember some of the more difficult moments, of course, but what we remember most is watching movies in the hospital together and the giant monkey balloon that Grandma Sheri (aka Shuie) brought us. We remember friends who came to visit and bring gifts and the feeling of knowing that the most important thing was being together. The doctors told us that the quickest recovery time they had ever seen was four days and that we should plan to be there for about ten days. Abby's surgery went so well, and she responded with such strength and energy, they sent us home on day four. We looked around at other kids that had been in the hospital for months, and we recognized how fortunate we were that Abby's surgery and recovery went so well. We prayed for those parents who were not as fortunate.

As we left the hospital, doctors told us that Abby would probably want to rest and be somewhat lethargic for several days. We were instructed to keep her from doing any strenuous activity and not allow anything that might jeopardize the stitches or open the wounds or damage the tender areas that were healing. After all, they had just cut into her chest, opened her heart, and stopped her lungs.

When our family arrived back home, we set up pillows and cushions on the couch for Abby with her favorite movie on the TV. Tyce and I were so exhausted that we left Abby's big brother, Caleb, to watch over her while we went to take a short nap. We were fully depending on the doctor's assumption that she would feel lethargic and would want to rest. Just as we were getting settled in for our nap, Caleb came running into our bedroom, yelling for us to come help with Abby. We bolted into the living room to find Abby jumping on the couch! Not only did she not want to rest, but the surgery resulted in giving her increased energy!

Though our nap would have to wait, we were overjoyed at Abby's recovery and successful surgery, and we thanked God for how He had blessed our family.

Abby has now grown into a young woman who is still delicate and tender but also strong and determined. She continues to over-come many challenges and exhibits a strength that she knows can only come from God. She relies on Him and trusts that He will continue to sustain her. As her parents, we are thankful to have a front-row view to what God is doing in her life. It has been such fun to watch as others recognize her gifts and abilities, and introduce us to opportunities for her to use them. Abby's two brothers, Caleb and Luke, love her deeply and have embraced their role as her protectors (and sometimes for fun they pretend to be her antagonists). God has taught us so much through Abby, and people often ask about the lessons we've learned and our unique experiences. It's our prayer that you'll be encouraged, comforted, and strengthened through reading this brief compilation of a few of our most memorable lessons and experiences.

 Blessed be the God and Father of our Lord Jesus Christ, the Father of mercies and God of all comfort, who comforts us in all our affliction, so that we may be able to comfort those who are in any affliction, with the comfort with which we ourselves are comforted by God. For as we share abundantly in Christ's sufferings, so through Christ we share abundantly in comfort too. If we are afflicted, it is for your comfort and salvation; and if we are comforted, it is for your comfort, which you experience when you patiently endure the same sufferings that we suffer. Our hope for you is unshaken, for we know that as you share in our sufferings, you will also share in our comfort.

— 2 Corinthians 1: 3–7

Chapter 1

Welcome to the Real World

Unplanned and Abnormal?

O r part of the plan and the reality of life?
We often tell people that we are an average family with some not- so-average experiences. We now have a sign in our kitchen that reads, "As far as anyone knows, we are a nice normal family." We all find this humorous because we know we're not "normal," if there even is such a thing as normal. Down syndrome is one of the main reasons why most people don't consider us to fit into what they consider normal. As you've hopefully read in the prologue and introduction, the little girl who had heart surgery at age five is our daughter Abby, and Abby has Down syndrome.

Heart surgery wasn't our first experience with medical concerns, though perhaps the most significant. Before Abby was born, routine sonograms showed that she wasn't growing as she should. My doctor recommended amniocentesis, but we declined. I had experienced three miscarriages already and knew that the test increased the risk of having another. We also knew the results of amniocentesis would not change our course of action. Abortion was not an option and never would be for us. There were indications that Abby may have some kind of chromosomal abnormality, but also the possibility that she was just really short. All her vital organs appeared healthy, and the doctor told us the test was not necessary, so we decided to hope for the best and assume she was simply vertically challenged. Neither my husband nor I are very tall. Maybe she just received all the short genes, since her big brother seemed to have received all the tall ones. This was how we joked, knowing that each child is unique and would have their own individual characteristics. Our older son, Caleb, had overcome his eight-weeks-premature birth to now be on the upper edge of the growth chart for height.

Because Caleb had arrived so prematurely, when I began having preterm labor with Abby at twenty-nine weeks, my doctor ordered me to strict bedrest. His exact instructions were two-minute showers and only getting up to use the bathroom or move from the couch to the bed. Caleb was an active two-year-old who had become accustomed to being with me almost all of the time. Suddenly, I was unable to walk with him to the park or take him to playdates with friends. This was how life with Abby began. We were careful with our words so Caleb would not resent the baby that kept Mom from playing with him. I was thankful for family members and others who came to help and many friends who brought us meals.

When my mother came for a visit, she wisely brought along a baby doll so Caleb could pretend to help care for the baby. We spoke to Caleb about what a good big brother he would be. When Abby was born, he loved her right away. He knew nothing about Down syndrome; only that he had a baby sister. I found myself wishing everyone else saw her as he did. I wondered how much different things might have been if we had never announced to friends and family that Abby had Down syndrome. Indeed, they would have noticed, but perhaps they would not have grieved for us to the extent they did.

While I was on bedrest, I had a lot of time to read. I was able to catch up on all the reading I had not finished as mom to a busy two-year-old. While other friends and family cared for Caleb, I devoured the stack of reading that I had set aside for the past two years. One of the articles I read during this time was about a family that had a child with Down syndrome. It described what a blessing this child was to their family. I set the article aside and moved on to the next, and I didn't realize that my expectations for my child and my future had just been changed. I later realized what a gift God provided when He led me to read that article. Instead of grieving at the news when Abby was born, I was able to view Down syndrome as a potential blessing.

Processing and Responding

Moments after she was born, I was relieved to find out that Abby's Apgar scores were good, and she appeared to be healthy. My husband later said that he remembers how the room went silent as soon as Abby arrived. The doctors and nurses could immediately see that Abby most likely had Down syndrome, but I was still clueless at that point. A few hours later, when I had rested a bit and finally received a meal, a doctor and intern who were present at her birth came into my hospital room. I was famished and more interested in the meal that had just been delivered than whatever it was they had to say. The intern proceeded to tell us that they suspected that Abby had Down syndrome, and they would order tests to determine definitively if their suspicions were correct. They left the room quickly, and I simply returned my attention to my meal. Remember, I was famished, and I had already concluded that Down syndrome could be a blessing. I was stopped short from eating when my husband, Tyce, began to tear up. I could see that he was visibly upset and very fatigued. I pushed aside my meal, and we held each other and talked.

Tyce has told me that this moment in the hospital was when his emotions met his recognition of the fact that Abby had Down syndrome. He remembers asking the sonogram technician in the weeks prior what the most likely outcome would be with the signs that were visible on the sonogram, and the technician told him that Down syndrome was the likely outcome. A few days after that sonogram, Tyce was out on a trip in Louisville, Kentucky. He had checked into his hotel but couldn't sleep. He got down on his knees and prayed, and for over an hour, he poured out his heart and argued with God. The impression or answer God gave him at that time was, "This is my will. This is how it is. You can go along with it, enjoy the ride and be blessed, or you can fight against it and continue to struggle."

Tyce didn't sleep well that night. When Abby was born, and the news became official, he felt the full impact of how much he had to learn and how much it would impact our lives. He processed in that moment what I processed over a much longer period of time.

Neither Tyce nor I had much experience at all with Down syndrome, and we had not spent any significant time with any individuals with Down syndrome. The small number of past experiences Tyce had had left him with a negative view of Down syndrome. As the leader of our family and a fighter pilot, he felt that he was supposed to always be in control.

Down syndrome was something he could not control. But the fact that he felt out of control led him to turn to God. As he turned to God, he realized that he didn't have to have all the answers right now, but that God would provide what was needed for each moment.

When we shared the news with our parents and our siblings, and then with other family and friends, we received a variety of responses. I was actually quite surprised by some of them, and I was completely unprepared. I wanted to celebrate the birth of my new baby. I wanted to enjoy this beautiful little girl that God had placed in my arms. When others stayed mired in the sadness and disappointment of the fact that Abby had Down syndrome, I actually became angry. I instinctively distanced myself from those who did not celebrate her, and I was thankful for those who did rejoice with me. My mother-in-law planned a "Sip 'N See" shortly after Abby was born, which was a wonderful time of celebrating Abby and introducing her to family friends. It was a beautiful expression of acceptance and joy that was very meaningful to me.

Other parents have told me that they had almost the opposite reaction upon hearing the news that their child has a disability. Some spent a significant amount of time grieving and became angry when others expected them to celebrate. The divorce rate among parents who have a child with Down syndrome is extremely high, and I can imagine that these differing responses may be one of the first experiences that can potentially drive couples apart. When parents receive news that their child has Down syndrome or any other such anomaly, they may react in a variety of ways. I've seen about as many different responses as there are families. Each one of us processes in our own unique way, and it's important for us to recognize that different responses are okay.

> Each one of us processes in our own unique way, and it's important for us to recognize that different responses are okay.

We all have different backgrounds, different amounts of knowledge, different personalities. If one parent responds differently than another, we should not attach any particular assumptions about the parent or convey any judgments on them with the reception of their response.

When we find that someone thinks differently than we do, we

can ask questions and explore their reasoning. We can view it as an adventure from which we can learn and gain understanding. Tyce and I have found that our differences can often lead us closer together rather than further apart, when we take the time to talk and learn to understand each other. Even though we come from different perspectives on many issues and have very different personalities, we found one common bond that has always held us together. We both valued Abby because we believe the Bible when it says that we are all created in the image of God and that He has a plan for our lives which He established before we were born. It is the foundation of God's Word that we established in our marriage from the beginning that has helped us find common ground.

It is the foundation of God's Word that we established in our marriage from the beginning that has helped us find common ground.

If you have recently found out that your child has some anomaly like Down syndrome, you may not know exactly how God is working in your marriage or your family, but you can pray and then trust in knowing that God gave you this child together and will provide everything you need to sustain you.

So God created man in his own image, in the image of God he created him; male and female he created them.

— Genesis 1:27

 For you formed my inward parts; you knitted me together in my mother's womb.

I praise you, for I am fearfully and wonderfully made.

Wonderful are your works; my soul knows it very well.

My frame was not hidden from you, when I was being made in secret, intricately woven in the depths of the earth. Your eyes saw my unformed substance; in your book were written, every one of them, the days that were formed for me, when as yet there was none of them.

— Psalm 139:13-16

 "For I know the plans I have for you," declares the Lord, "plans for welfare and not for evil, to give you a future and a hope."

— Jeremiah 29:11

No Need to Be an Expert, Just Know Your Child

In the first few weeks of Abby's life, I attempted to learn as much information as I could about Down syndrome. I read books and articles and sought out organizations that provided resources and help. Some of the information that is widely published about Down syndrome includes these facts:

There are three forms of Down syndrome: Trisomy-21 (an extra 21st chromosome), Mosaic (a mixture of cells with 46 and 47 chromosomes), and Translocation (where the extra 21st chromosome attaches to another chromosome).

There are no known factors that cause Down syndrome. Down syndrome happens in all ethnic groups, across all socioeconomic levels, and is generally not hereditary. There is no known link to actions of the parents or environmental factors, and aside from an increased incidence as maternal age increases there are no risk indicators.

People with Down syndrome have some tendencies to have other medical issues, such as heart defects, respiratory difficulties, digestive problems, etc. They also tend to have mild to moderate cognitive impairment and some difficulty with short and/or long-term memory. Most of us recognize the common physical characteristics that are associated with Down syndrome, such as a flattened face and almond shaped eyes.

As I began to research all the possible effects and complications that might come with Abby having Down syndrome, I started feeling somewhat anxious and tried to brace myself for every possible negative scenario. I have a tendency to want to prepare for the worst. Before Abby was born, I had prepared myself for the worst possibility that I could imagine. I anticipated the most horrible scenario of having a child die at birth, so when I was told Abby was healthy, I was happy and relieved. But this tendency to ready myself for the worst was causing difficulty, because there were so many potential complications and no way of knowing which might affect our family. When I took Abby to visit our pediatrician, he noticed this anxiety in me. He wisely advised me to "just love her."

He reminded me that she is a child first of all, and he helped me put into perspective all the potential concerns that might arise. We would deal with them as they came, and most would never come. What he knew she needed right now is a mother who loved her. I'm so thankful for his wisdom. I began to focus on Abby, to learn to know her personality, to learn to love her and to enjoy who God created her to be. I didn't need to know what might come tomorrow, only enough to love her today.

> And why are you anxious about clothing? Consider the lilies of the field, how they grow: they neither toil nor spin, yet I tell you, even Solomon in all his glory was not arrayed like one of these. But if God so clothes the grass of the field, which today is alive and tomorrow is thrown into the oven, will he not much more clothe you, O you of little faith? Therefore do not be anxious, saying, "What shall we eat?" or "What shall we drink?" or "What shall we wear?" For the Gentiles seek after all these things, and your heavenly Father knows that you need them all. But seek first the kingdom of God and his righteousness, and all these things will be added to you. Therefore do not be anxious about tomorrow, for tomorrow will be anxious for itself. Sufficient for the day is its own trouble.
>
> — Matthew 6:28-34

Don't Focus on the Diagnosis

Tyce remembers how he avoided reading information about Down syndrome because he found so much of it was negative. The focus on the negative was causing him to view Abby as a problem that needed to be fixed rather than a child that needed to be loved. While additional information can be helpful at times, there is also wisdom in avoiding too much negative information. Thankfully, we

17

realized that we didn't need to be experts on Down syndrome. We just needed to learn to know Abby. We had to let go of our preconceived ideas about Down syndrome and about what our daughter would be like and instead fully embrace, accept, and learn to love the daughter God gave us.

Abby is not "broken" because she has Down syndrome. Some call Down syndrome a disorder. Some call it a disability. Some call it a problem. I call it an anomaly. Abby's life is not out of order or broken. She is not a problem, and she is fully capable of functioning and exhibiting many normal abilities. An anomaly is defined as "something that deviates from what is standard, normal, or expected." There may even be a better word, but Down syndrome is a deviation from what is standard and is usually not expected. And none of us are really "normal," so there's that. I believe God likes variety. Visit the zoo and you simply can't deny that God is creative and exhibits amazing variety in creation. I think of Down syndrome as one of the exciting ways God decided to add variety to the human existence. Just as God gave some individuals red hair or big noses, He gave Abby Down syndrome. It is a small part of what makes Abby unique and is an aspect of her character that endears many to her. Down syndrome is also a way in which God can be glorified in her life. You'll read more about this in the chapter on "The End of the Matter, When All Has Been Heard."

Some call it a disability.
Some call it a problem.
I call it an anomaly.

David Egan wrote a book titled *More Alike Than Different,*[1] in which he describes his life with Down syndrome. I love the title of the book, reminding us that people with Down syndrome have more in common with others than they have differences. Every individual is unique and complex, including those with Down syndrome.

When I say that Abby is not "broken," I am in no way ignoring the obvious challenges that come with Down syndrome. I recognize that Abby may need more time to learn new things or complete certain tasks. She also forgets some of what she has learned if she doesn't use it regularly. (Don't we all? I think I've forgotten everything I learned in calculus.) But because Abby is my daughter, I am learning to look at life through a different lens. Did she need to remember all those things? So often she helps remind me of what is really important.

Abby loves to read the Bible, sing songs of praise and worship to God, and meditate on and memorize Scripture. She would spend every day, all day, focused on these things and sharing God's love with others if she could. We often struggled when we believed she needed to learn math or history or science, and we had to pull her way from her Bible to teach some other subject. We questioned ourselves every time we commanded, "Abby, put away your Bible and do your schoolwork." I have come to think that perhaps she can learn all the science and math she needs to know from studying the Bible alone. I continue to be amazed at how much truth is in the Bible that we don't even recognize is there. The Bible is not anti-science but displays the foundations of science. It contains lessons for math, art, literature… every subject can be addressed through study of Scripture.

Abby achieved an eighth-grade level of education when she was seventeen years old, and the work was very time-consuming for her. She had the cognitive ability to continue and participate in further formal academics, but it consumed almost every moment of her day to complete the assignments for classes at her level of learning. (This is discussed in greater detail in the section on Scaling Schoolwork.)

We saw frustration building in her, as she desired to spend her time reading and learning from God's Word instead of memorizing the location of countries on the other side of the world and such.

Is it okay to spend all day focusing on God and the Bible? Isn't there laundry and cooking to be done, bills to pay, and other work we must do? Yes, of course. Can we focus on God while also accomplishing the tasks that need to be completed? This is a struggle we encounter on a daily basis. I tend to be so task oriented that I often forget about people and just zoom by them to get to the next task on my list. Ask my husband and he will verify that I often look right past him when I'm intent on completing some work. But Abby is completely God-oriented and people-oriented.

My life is better because Abby has Down syndrome, and this is one of the reasons why. Abby helps me slow down, pay attention to people, and spend more time focusing on and listening to God. She helps me find balance and inspiration for appropriate focus on God, His Word, and the people around me, while also still moving forward to accomplish tasks.

I'm learning, largely through Abby's influence in my life, that it IS possible to focus on God while still accomplishing needed tasks.

Unless the Lord builds the house, those who build it labor in vain. Unless the Lord watches over the city, the watchman stays awake in vain. It is in vain that you rise up early and go late to rest, eating the bread of anxious toil; for he gives to his beloved sleep.

— Psalm 127:1-2

His divine power has granted to us all things that
pertain to life and godliness, through the knowledge
of him who called us to his own glory and excellence.

— 2 Peter 1:3

 All scripture is breathed out by God and profitable for
teaching, for reproof, for correction, and for training
in righteousness, that the man of God may be
complete, equipped for every good work.

— 2 Timothy 3:16-17

Developing Valuable Character Qualities: i.e., Practicing Patience

I don't always want to slow down. Because I am often task oriented,
I also tend to be impatient. I'm amazed how many people say, "Oh,
you have a child with Down syndrome. You must be a very patient
person." Well, I'm not patient by nature. But I am learning to practice patience more often. Because I love Abby, I have often made
the choice to practice patience. But if you'll notice, I didn't say that
I have mastered the skill of being patient. When I focus on love,
when I seek God's direction and keep my mind focused on what I
know is right and good, I make the choice to practice patience. But
if I fail to focus on love, I find myself easily reverting to my natural
tendency to be impatient.

Because I love Abby, I have often made the choice to practice patience. But if you'll notice, I didn't say that I have mastered the skill of being patient.

I remember a prayer I whispered to God when I was young, asking that God would help me be more patient because I knew it was a valuable character quality and something I needed to increase in my life. Perhaps Abby is an answer to that prayer. I see God using Abby to help everyone around her practice patience and develop self-control. She has been very instrumental in helping each member of our family grow and learn to live by the Spirit as is described in Galatians 5:22–26.

Those who know Abby or who work with her for a time tell us they learn from her and benefit greatly from time spent with her. For many years, Abby attended an overnight camp during the first week of summer break. Every time we would pick her up from camp, we would hear stories of how she impacted the counselors and campers and staff. Many times, counselors would share what they learned from her with tears in their eyes. Abby often has a profound effect on others and can demonstrate God's love in unique ways. She introduces us to new ways of thinking and responding to our everyday situations. She often challenges the expectations and assumptions that we often don't even realize we possess.

♥ 💜 ♥

But the fruit of the Spirit is love, joy, peace, patience, kindness, goodness, faithfulness, gentleness, self-control; against such things there is no law. And those who belong to Christ Jesus have crucified the flesh with its passions and desires. If we live by the Spirit, let us also keep in step with the Spirit. Let us not become conceited, provoking one another, envying one another.

— Galatians 5:22-26

Why Not Me? Changing Expectations

It seems unavoidable for parents to have expectations about how their child will look and behave, what they will be like, even from before birth. Many parents read the book *What to Expect When You're Expecting.*[2] We're expecting certain things when we anticipate the arrival of a child.

I remember literally having dreams at night about what my first child would look like. Anytime we have expectations that are not met, there will be a process of grieving or expressing the frustration that inevitably results.

I too read the *What to Expect When You're Expecting* book. I read the small section about Down syndrome and other anomalies that were possible. I think we have a tendency to skip right over those parts and assume that it will always be someone else who has to deal with those issues, and that's basically what I did. However, the abnormal sonogram results, along with the article I had read about Down syndrome and the fact that I didn't know anyone who had Down syndrome, caused me to take some pause. These factors together led me to think that statistically, Down syndrome might be a possibility for us. I remember telling my husband somewhere along the way, "We don't know anyone who has a child with Down syndrome. Why wouldn't it be us?" I don't think he enjoyed that thought. After Abby was born, I read the statistic that about 1 in 1,200 pregnancies is a child with Down syndrome. Instead of asking the question, "Why me?" I asked the question, "Why not me?" At about the same time, I happened to read that the probability of finding a four- leaf clover was about the same. I began calling Abby "my little four-leaf clover." I wrote a song for Abby around that time that includes these words: "You are my four-leaf clover. How lucky I am to have you in my life." I recently recorded it and made it available for others to hear. (You can find a link to it at the end of the book under "For More Information.")

There is a story that has circulated for years among parents who have a child born with some disability. It's called *"Welcome to Holland"* and is written by Emily Perl Kingsley.[3] It is a story of someone who was planning to go to Italy and had made all the preparations to visit the beautiful land of Italy and enjoy all the wonderful sights to see there. But instead of landing in Italy, they found they'd been rerouted to Holland. The story is essentially a lament of lost expectations, of a dream that was not realized, of hopes that did not materialize. While it seems that everyone else is going to "Italy," those who have a child with a disability are rerouted to "Holland."

What I've come to realize is that going to "Holland" is not any less desirable. In fact, for me, having a child with Down syndrome is better. Who told me that I was going to Italy anyway? If I had attempted to avoid being rerouted to "Holland," I would have missed out on God's wonderful plan for me. I've come to understand that God's plan for me is better than anything I could have planned for myself. As a result, I can enjoy my trip to "Holland" and all that comes with having a child with Down syndrome. I could continue to grieve all along the way, and admittedly, there are times when I still do, but if I waste my time grieving, I may miss out on all the joy that this new destination has to offer. If you spend all your time in Holland thinking about what you missed out on in Italy, then you also miss enjoying all the beauty that Holland has to offer. Why not enjoy the windmills and tulips and all the unique features that can be found in Holland? Why not learn to enjoy the blessings that come with having a child with Down syndrome? We have taught Abby's brothers about the benefits that they receive from having her as their sister. There are many lessons our family has learned that we probably would not have learned if Abby did not have Down syndrome. What the world sees as something that could harm or destroy us, God uses for our good.

You may recall a verse in Genesis 37, amid the account of Joseph and his family conflict, after he had been sold into slavery by his brothers. Joseph continued to trust God despite his circumstances, and God used all the trials in his life for good. God redeems what we see as broken or painful in this world and makes something beautiful from it.

We tend to go through life with the usual expectations of getting married, adopting a pet, having children, buying a home, our kids progressing through school and going to college, moving out on their own, and so on. I had all these same expectations, but I have now begun to question how many of these expectations are unrealistic or even unnecessary. There are certain patterns to life, yes, and setting goals is profitable, but not everyone follows the same patterns. Some people remain single. Some couples never have children. Some kids never go to college. Some never move away from home.

There are certain patterns to life,
yes, and setting goals is profitable,
but not everyone follows
the same patterns.

I am learning to look to God and wait for Him to lead rather than looking to the world and trying to make things happen by myself. I haven't mastered this by any means. I still hope for grand-kids someday! But I'm not going to manipulate the lives of my children to acquire my expectations and fulfill the plan I have in mind. God's plan is always best, so I choose to wait and see what He has in store and rest in knowing that it will be better than anything I could have arranged on my own.

Even if I am never blessed to have grandchildren, I can have peace knowing that God's plan is best. God commands us in Psalm 46:10 to "Be still, and know that I am God." When you allow God to work in your life, as He has already planned to do, you can watch in amazement as He is glorified in the unique story that plays out through you.

 For Further Reflection

- What does it mean to be a normal person or a normal family?
- What preconceived ideas have you possessed about Down syndrome?
- How have your past experiences impacted your thoughts about Down syndrome or other such anomalies?
- Do you see ways that Down syndrome can be a blessing?
- Have you seen examples in your life of how difficulties produced something good?
- Do you struggle to find an appropriate balance between focusing on God and His Word, other people around you, and the tasks you need to accomplish?
- In what ways can you find common ground with others when they respond differently to circumstances affecting you?
- Have you experienced times in your life when you felt out of control? How did you respond?
- What expectations do you have for your future or your child's future? What is your natural response to unmet expectations?
- How do verses such as Genesis 1:27 and Psalm 139 influence your view of yourself and others?

Chapter 2

Communicate, Delegate, and Relate

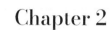

Y ou probably already recognize the significance of communication in relationships where two or more people must work together in unity, or at least in harmony, to accomplish certain goals. Those who are married can no doubt attest to the fact that communication is an important aspect of a healthy marriage. When our son Caleb first became involved in a significant dating relationship, we began talking with him more often about marriage. One such conversation became an ongoing joke in our home. Caleb had observed a moment of confusion between Tyce and me, and he probably recognized for the first time that these moments of confusion happen quite frequently in our relationship. After this minor miscommunication was resolved, Caleb lightheartedly asked both Tyce and me, "Is marriage just one big failure to communicate?" My immediate response was a resounding, "Yes!" At the exact same moment, however, Tyce responded with a more hesitant "No..." Because we all found humor in this situation, whenever we have some miscommunication or a moment of confusion, it is common for us to refer back to this discussion and once again laugh at the ongoing challenges of communicating and how we sometimes respond with distinctly opposing views.

Tyce and I communicate using quite different methods. Communication is one of those areas where we notice the huge discrepancies between his fighter pilot background and my pacifist tendencies. He attacks conflict head-on, while I tend to avoid conflict whenever possible. We learned at a Family Life Weekend to Remember conference that these are labeled as the "fight or flight" responses. We were opposites in regard to this aspect of communication. We began to recognize more clearly that there are various ways of communicating and that each person we interact with comes from a different background. You may know some people who are much more cautious and careful with their words, but you may also have friends who are boisterous and have little concern for the way their words will be interpreted. You may have a friend who processes information by talking out loud or another friend who becomes quiet and contemplative or wants to be alone when thinking through an issue.

Communication between two people in marriage can be difficult enough, but when, as parents, we work with additional people to meet our child's needs, we sometimes experience even greater challenges.

As Tyce and I have enlisted others to help us achieve goals we have set for Abby, including some individuals who might have significantly differing communication styles and habits, we have been required to navigate various aspects of communication in very personal aspects of our lives. As we have worked with therapists, educators, and others who served in some role of helping Abby, we have discovered new ways to communicate. We've come to recognize the impact of the way we interact, the importance of the words we use, and the need to define roles and clarify responsibilities.

A Parent's Role in Therapy—Interact and Implement

Tyce often tells a story of teaching Abby about colors. He began repeating the same lesson to her for what felt like the millionth time, thinking how it seemed she would never learn it. Then one day, he heard her reciting the colors all by herself! She had learned it! Teaching Abby has been like that all along the way. Sometimes, you catch that moment when the light bulb comes on and your child "gets it," but often, you just keep going at the same task until one day you realize she's ready to move on. We have chosen to participate in Abby's learning as often as possible. We catch a few more of those "aha!" moments because we participate.

We've had many therapists in our home over the years, working with Abby on physical therapy, speech therapy, oral motor therapy, occupational therapy, sensory integration therapy, etc. Each type of therapy targeted a particular set of muscles or tasks that we were helping Abby develop. We often had two or three types of therapy appointments in our weekly schedule, but usually not more than three at a time. Many of the therapists told us that they could see a significant difference in Abby because we engaged in helping administer therapy activities with her on a daily basis. Both Tyce and I took the time to watch the therapy when we could and learned how to do the activities on our own with her.

We had known virtually nothing about any of these types of therapy before Abby was born. At one appointment, when Abby was very young and just beginning a new type of therapy, Tyce was watching and noticed that the therapist was simply playing in a specific way with specific goals in mind. He commented to the therapist that the activities themselves did not require any special training but simply a thoughtful engagement in being aware of Abby's needs. The therapist agreed and told him that any kind of purposeful play was helpful. As busy parents, this was so encouraging for us to recognize. While there was a benefit to learning about various muscles and the specific exercises that would target specific strengthening, we didn't have to know everything about physical therapy or occupational therapy or oral motor therapy. We primarily just needed to pay attention to Abby and engage with her in positive ways.

> We didn't have to know everything about physical therapy or occupational therapy or oral motor therapy. We primarily just needed to pay attention to Abby.

So much of education is simply recognizing the needs of the child. While professional educators and therapists often learn specific techniques, targeted programs and best practices for meeting a particular goal, the key often is knowing how to apply those techniques and programs and practices with each individual child. This is where parents must be involved to help therapy be truly effective. As Tyce and I watched the therapists and talked with them about Abby, we learned together how to fit the techniques and practices to Abby's specific needs. We learned how to implement new practices and introduce new patterns into our daily routine. Communication with the therapists was an essential part of Abby's progress.

This communication did require a great deal of time from us as parents. We could not just allow the therapist to come in and work with Abby while we attended to other tasks. When we valued the therapist as much as the therapy, and we demonstrated our appreciation for their expertise, they were happy to share more information with us and work to better understand Abby. I think it also made their work more enjoyable as they saw greater results from the time spent with her. Many workers have expressed to us how they enjoyed coming into our home and seeing Abby.

Most everyone recognizes a certain joy when parents engage in teaching and guiding their children. We instinctively know that it is wholesome and good and right for parents to be active and engaged with their kids, in training and directing and leading them, in communicating with them in healthy ways.

As parents, we know this is true, but when we are in the midst of training our child, we can often fail to see the importance of our efforts. We may fail to recognize that the extra effort and time spent with them is valuable and will produce a good result. Why do we so often believe there is other more important work to be done when we know the value of a parent engaging with their child? Certain factors prevalent in our society have trained us to believe a lie. We are often told that working with children is something anyone can do, but is it? Perhaps anyone can tell a child what to do and force them to do certain activities, but not everyone is wise enough or aware enough to recognize the deeper needs of the individual child. If you had caregivers who were unaware of your needs as a child, you likely know what I mean.

Tyce and I wanted to always be aware of the needs of our kids, to strive to meet their needs, to help them reach their full potential. A therapist or teacher who only interacts for several hours each week with each child cannot devote the same attention that a parent can, no matter how kind and loving the therapist or teacher may be. Certainly, they can recognize certain things and give helpful guidance, as many therapists did for Abby. But they cannot observe the whole of her life, bring every aspect together, and view the specific task needed within the framework of the whole family and how it functions. It is our responsibility as parents to know our kids and guide their development. We cannot abdicate this responsibility to others. Instead, we should receive it with joy and view it as a gift and privilege, knowing it is right and good to fulfill our role as parents.

It is our responsibility as parents to know our kids and guide their development. We cannot abdicate this responsibility to others.

When we engage in intentional communication with those who work with our kids, and we make the effort to interact with them and implement what we learn, our whole family and the community around us all benefit.

Behold, children are a heritage from the Lord, the fruit of the womb a reward. Like arrows in the hands of a warrior are the children of one's youth. Blessed is the man who fills his quiver with them!

— Psalm 127:3-5

Values on Display

Therapists and workers who come into your home will not understand everything about your child and your family, but they do make many observations. When workers come into your home regularly, they have a front-row view of how you live. They see whether you live out what you profess to believe. They observe what you truly value. They also can have influence and change the course of your lives if you allow them to do so, for better or worse.

It can be challenging to find workers who have values that align with your own or who at least recognize, respect and honor the values you establish in your home. It can be a tricky process to navigate, and we learned that we had to be very careful about how we communicated our values to the people who came into our home regularly to work with Abby.

We have tried to teach with gentleness the standards we strive to hold to, without imposing our own convictions onto others or expecting them to change. Establishing our authority over our home with workers has been essential in our communication. The idealistic mindset of a young worker may need to be met with the wisdom that comes from the experience of the parents. At the same time, we recognize that we can learn new things and grow from our interaction with someone new who truly cares for our daughter.

Tyce and I had read from many respected sources that it is important for families to eat meals together regularly. For our family, meals together happen at any time of day. We don't have a consistent routine due to the odd hours of Tyce's job as an airline pilot. Some days, he leaves for work at 3 a.m. and returns three days later at noon. On other days, he leaves at 3 p.m., then returns home the next night at midnight. We purposefully adjust our activities at home to include Tyce whenever possible, so we have grown accustomed to eating meals together at any hour of the day. Last week, Tyce returned home from a difficult trip at 10:30 p.m. He was hungry, and the rest of us had eaten a very light snack that evening, so we all had dinner together at 10:30 p.m. We do try to have some structure in spite of such odd work hours, but including Tyce in our lives takes priority over maintaining structure. We see now how God has helped us all learn to be flexible, where we may have otherwise had a tendency to be too rigid.

Those who come into our home observe that we eat meals together at odd times. They observe how we have discussions throughout the day. They may think we are lazy at times when we sleep in after a previously late night. They may observe our actions but not know the reason behind the actions. Sometimes, I take time to explain our priorities and the reasons for certain oddities in our home to those who come to help. Other times I don't explain, and I hope they give grace and withhold making too many judgments. I don't concern myself too much if they do.

We communicate our values in a variety of ways, sometimes better than others. But also, certain values are more important than others for us to communicate. When others come into our home, they see the books we read and the movies we watch; they hear the music we listen to and the way we speak to each other, and sometimes, it is important for us to explain why we allow some things in our home and not others. Others don't always agree with our choices.

We have been tremendously blessed to have several women who have worked with Abby and come into our home on a weekly basis who became like family to us. The relationship we've had with them was mutually beneficial. Several of these young women now have children of their own, and I'm praying that they will be encouraged by reading this book and knowing that they have had a significant impact on helping Abby to grow and meeting the needs of our family. We are so thankful that God provided these women to help us, and that they were obedient to God's call in their lives. It is such a joy to observe how they are using everything they have learned, to see them continuing to grow and continuing to have a tremendous impact on others.

♥ ♥ ♥

Therefore encourage one another and build one
another up, just as you are doing.

— 1 Thessalonians 5:11

The Opinions That Really Matter

As a result of having a child with Down syndrome, we have learned
not to concern ourselves too much with what other people think.
We know there is a stigma associated with Down syndrome. We
know some people can be mean. Any unique need or characteristic
can bring out either the worst or best in others. We know people
watch Abby and watch how we interact with her. Sometimes, in
public places, I think about this and make a purposeful effort to
show others that I value her and enjoy her. But usually, we simply
live our lives without concern for how others interpret our actions.
We have found that people who really care and are interested in
knowing Abby will approach us. We've met some beautiful people
with very kind hearts. Abby has some of the best friends, and we
have come to know some of the sweetest young women because
Abby has Down syndrome.

We've also met some people who were not so kind towards
Abby or our family. Of course, I have felt frustration and sometimes
anger. But as I learned to overcome my own feelings of hurt, it
wasn't very long before I began to grieve more for others who
wouldn't accept Abby than for myself or my family. I recognize that
those who reject Abby because she has Down syndrome are
harming themselves with this choice, and I don't need to allow
them to also harm our family.

When we moved into a new neighborhood, we attended a play-
date with neighborhood children of similar ages, hoping to make
some new friends. We received comments that made it clear we
were not accepted into the group. We would have had to make

drastic changes if we wanted to be welcomed among that circle of families, and even then, I wasn't confident that we would be accepted. I was not willing to make significant changes to our lives in an attempt to receive the approval of my new neighbors and possibly be accepted into that circle of women. I wonder now how much different those children's lives may have been if their parents had been more open to welcoming Abby as a friend. Perhaps I should have worked harder to convince our neighbors of the benefits of knowing Abby and having her as a friend for their child, but I didn't want to force someone to value her or engage in what they saw as an obligatory relationship. We moved on to seek out other friendships, and we have always appreciated those friends who recognized Abby's value and accepted us from the beginning.

We have always appreciated those friends who recognized Abby's value and accepted us from the beginning.

The young women who have genuinely befriended Abby tend to have similar characteristics. They are kind, gentle, selfless, generous, curious, and adventurous. They are the kind of women I hope my sons might marry someday. The way someone interacts with Abby is a good indicator of their true character. We have seen some girls who wanted to make themselves feel better or look more attractive by spending time with Abby. Others ignore Abby and just don't want to think about the fact that she is different, or perhaps they don't even notice that she is different but are not drawn to her. Others can be downright mean. We have tried to protect Abby from the people who are mean or who demonstrate openly that they don't value her because she has Down syndrome. I know Abby has felt ignored at times, but we are thankful that she has not had significant experiences where others have hurt her clearly and directly.

As Abby has ventured out more on her own as an adult, she is often asked about her experiences. Sometimes it seems that she portrays the hurt that she has seen happen to others as if it has happened to her. She has such a heart of empathy that when her friends are hurt and she hears about their experience, she takes it upon herself as her own pain. Because her memory of past events is not clear, she sometimes repeats what others tell her about her past. She knows she spent time in public school and she sometimes describes feeling rejected and treated differently in public school because she has Down syndrome, but the reality is that she was only three years old when that happened. She feels this rejection because she has heard her parents talk about it. We have to be careful about how we describe our experiences with her and make sure she doesn't receive these experiences as something that changes her attitude and understanding of who she really is. We have always taught her that she is valuable and loved, and we strive to ensure that she continues to hear that message more loudly than she hears the message about how others rejected her.

Abby is confident in her value as a child of God, but she still cares what others think of her. We have tried to avoid placing much emphasis on outward appearance. As Abby has stepped into the role of being a public speaker, it has been more difficult to avoid focusing on appearance.

Because Abby chooses to be in the spotlight and onstage, she must find a healthy balance in this area. We recognize how challenging it can be to avoid the emphasis on outward appearance. One of Abby's strengths is her innocence and pure heart. We hope to keep her from being distracted by being overly concerned about outward appearance or surface-level issues. We have seen that Abby's simplicity often allows others to let their guard down and move past the exterior to focus on heart issues. Her dad tells her she is beautiful just as she is, without needing makeup or anything fancy to enhance her appearance. She knows she is loved for who she is on the inside and not simply how she looks on the outside. This is a truth that is not commonly understood among most young women but is extremely important for them to grasp.

I remember reading an article about a couple who had adopted several children with special needs. The author of the article commented to the parents during the interview, stating that each of the children was beautiful in their own way. One of the parents responded by saying, "They are not loved because they are beautiful. They are beautiful because they are loved." I find this to be true in many relationships. We are all loved by God. The more we understand that truth, the more beauty we exhibit or portray to others.

We are all loved by God.
The more we understand that
truth, the more beauty we exhibit
or portray to others.

Much of what we know to be true beauty is what is found inside rather than what we see on the outside. Perhaps you can think of someone who may externally be beautiful and considered attractive to many, but you find them ugly because of what you have seen in their actions. As God told Samuel in 1 Samuel 16:7, "Man looks on the outward appearance, but the LORD looks on the heart." Because Abby is so firmly convinced that she is immensely loved by God, she exhibits a depth of beauty in her character that I and others greatly admire.

❤ 🤍 ❤

> And do not fear those who kill the body but cannot kill the soul. Rather fear him who can destroy both soul and body in hell.

— Matthew 10:28

Accuracy in Evaluations

Another blessing of Abby having Down syndrome is that it is visibly obvious to others. When people meet her, there is often an immediate response that can indicate to us how much emphasis they place on outward appearance or cognitive ability. When we are wise and observe, we can use this information to help others learn.

We all make assumptions based on outward appearance. Observations based on outward appearance can help us understand a person to a degree but making too many assumptions can be harmful. Many people make too many assumptions about Abby based on her outward appearance. These assumptions can create difficulty when we need to obtain an accurate evaluation of Abby's abilities. Assumptions are particularly common when in larger groups. The need to organize and categorize can lead to labels and segregation. We were confronted with this lesson when our kids entered the world of formal education.

Tyce and I were both educated primarily in public schools, and as young parents, we knew next to nothing about homeschooling. We began our family with the assumption that our kids would attend full-time school as we did. When our kids were little, and I spent my days wiping bottoms, noses, and countertops (usually not with the same cloth, and if so, definitely not in that order!), I looked forward to the day when my kids would all be in school and I would have time to develop my own interests once again.

Through my years in public school, I learned to value independence. I learned to be competitive, to look out for myself, to strive to achieve success. I strongly identify with a statement that I hear my husband often declare: "When I got married, I realized how selfish I had been. When I had kids, I realized how lazy I had been." Even though I recognized that selfishness and laziness were undesirable character qualities, my natural desire was still to go back to the more selfish and lazy way of life as soon as possible. This natural desire and heart attitude were essentially what led us to pursue full-time schooling for our kids.

When it was time to begin formal education for our kids, we placed Caleb in the best private school we could find, and when Abby was old enough to qualify, we enrolled her in public school and anticipated that the school administrators would know best how to meet her needs. We had been told that our school district was one of the better districts for providing services for kids with special needs. We entered the process with high hopes and engaged with teachers and administrators with the belief that they would know how to direct us to meet Abby's educational needs.

On the day we arrived at the school for Abby's initial assessment, we were directed into a tiny room that was packed full of supplies, basically the supply closet for that particular elementary school. They asked us to sit at the small table made for children and began to ask me questions about Abby's abilities while they brought out various toys and other items. I was completely unprepared for the encounter and had no idea what to expect. I answered the questions to the best of my knowledge. They asked Abby to perform a few tasks without giving her much instruction or time to complete them. The evaluation was fairly short, and the school staff all seemed friendly. When we received the analysis that they had created summarizing Abby's abilities, we were very surprised. When we received their recommendation for placement, we were even more surprised.

They intended to place Abby in a small classroom with only a handful of other children who all had special needs. They had chosen to focus on the things Abby could not do, and it appeared to me that they had discarded any information about Abby's strengths and abilities. They made a determination of how she should be educated based on a very short encounter with her. They placed labels on her and put her into categories, based on what programs they already had available rather than considering what she really needed. I am thankful that I had spent enough time with Abby to recognize her abilities and how the school had failed to make an accurate evaluation of her.

My friend Geri Green described to me an experience she had when taking her daughter Emily for a similar kind of evaluation: "When Emily was starting kindergarten, the public school she attended was quick to determine that she needed special education services like physical therapy, occupational therapy, vision therapy, etc. For each service, she had to undergo testing so needs could be identified and goals could be written. One morning, I drove Emily to a different school so the speech/ language pathologist could evaluate her. Carol (the pathologist, whom we had never met) introduced herself, talked with us for a moment or two, and then led Emily back to her office for testing. I waited anxiously in the lobby. After all, these situations rarely yield good news or congratulations for parents. When Carol brought Emily back out to the lobby, Carol had tears in her eyes. I wasn't quite sure what to make of that! She told me Emily had done very well, they had enjoyed their time together, and we would go over the results at the upcoming IEP meeting. (An IEP is an Individualized Education Plan. Every student who receives special education services in a public school has this document which states the current abilities of the student and lists all the goals the student will work toward in the coming year.)

A few days later, I got a note in the mail from Carol. I was expecting it to be information regarding Emily's speech/language evaluation, but instead I found an explanation for the tears that had been in Carol's eyes the morning she did Emily's evaluation. Carol wrote that her husband had passed away recently, and she missed him very much. The day she worked with Emily had been Carol's birthday, and she had been feeling sorry for herself because her husband was gone, and she had no one to celebrate with. Then Carol said that, as they wrapped up the evaluation, for no apparent reason, Emily started singing "Happy Birthday to Carol." Carol wrote that for her, it was 'a total God moment, as there was no way Emily could've known' it was her birthday or how much she needed 'to hear from Him.' Of course, reading Carol's note brought tears to my eyes. To me, this story is an example of how God can use anyone, if we are willing to be moved by the Spirit."

Start Somewhere

After receiving the results of the public-school evaluation, I began to ask questions. I began to meet other parents. I began to learn so much more about our public education system and special needs programs than I ever thought I wanted to know. I found that we were not alone in our feelings of disappointment in the public-school special programs. Many parents in our community shared with me their frustration and negative experiences. I began to engage in a fight for our daughter, to be her advocate and find others who would also be advocates for her. I also began to help advocate for other students in our community. I had much to learn, but I felt confident that school policies and procedures needed to change.

I had read about other schools that were implementing inclusive practices, and I had already seen how important it was for Abby to have positive peer models. I knew that Abby had the ability to participate in a classroom with typical-developing students, and I knew that the segregated classrooms they proposed would be harmful to her. It was obvious to me that their evaluation of Abby was incorrect, and their recommendations were not even close to what we had hoped would be provided. Our goals for Abby were much different than theirs.

One of the most important aspects of educating a child is correctly evaluating the child's current ability level. As we worked with school administrators and other professionals, we received assessments that we believed were inaccurate, or at best, incomplete. We were informed of other organizations where we could go for private evaluations that might be more comprehensive. We could purchase our own private evaluation and submit it to the school if we wanted administrators to make changes or at least consider additional information. Without any other evaluations, the school based it's recommendations for Abby's placement on this brief encounter with us and on the handful of questions we had answered.

I understand that schools have limited time and resources, and funding and allocation of resources is a completely different discussion that we could explore in depth. Tyce and I came to recognize that the public- school administrators had the option to allocate more funding for special programs if they valued them more highly. We came to understand that these processes and choices of administrators were essentially a reflection of the values that were prevalent in our community. Our district superintendent directly informed me of this fact during a private meeting I had requested with him. If you are familiar with Texas and the love of sports (especially football) that exists here, you might understand what the superintendent perceived to be the priorities for funding in our community and where discretionary funds are often distributed.

The public-school staff, such as special-program directors and diagnosticians, chose to make quick assessments and place students in the very small number of categories they had established as a reflection of the perceived values of the community. Decisions were made quickly, without fully considering the value of the individual child or accurately assessing their needs and abilities. I don't know whether these staff members had an end goal in mind for Abby's future, but if they did, it was clearly much different than the end goal we had in mind for her. While they may not have had a final goal in mind that we could agree to, I understand that they had to start somewhere and present to us the available services they were able to offer. Abby was merely one student among the many they were tasked with educating. To extend any additional effort to meet her needs would require that they begin to extend additional effort to other students as well. While we repeatedly asked them to consider better options for Abby and other students like her, they were unwilling to make more significant attempts to ensure her progress and success. They simply started with what they knew they could provide at the moment, which was a segregated classroom that I think we all knew was not what was really best for Abby.

Tyce and I also had to start somewhere. We began to understand that we didn't need to know everything. Our assessment of Abby didn't have to be fully accurate and complete. As her parents, we already knew more about her development, skills, abilities, and weaknesses than anyone else. We only needed to identify the right place to start. Our experience with Abby has helped us learn to take one step at a time. We can have an end goal in mind, but we may not know how to get there. Working with Abby often involves breaking down larger tasks into much smaller pieces. This has been a skill that has been valuable for me to learn. With our sons, we struggled with getting them to write out their math problems rather than just doing them quickly in their head. They were happy to skip steps and jump right to the solution. Abby forces us all to look at each step along the way, and I've come to recognize that can be a good thing. When evaluating a child's ability level and how to move forward, it's important to identify where they are in the process of learning and exactly which step of the process needs to be addressed next.

So often, I want to plan far ahead and look way into the future. I think I should be able to skip steps along the way to get where I want to go more quickly, but Abby helps me realize that each step is important. God often wants us to learn from each step along the way and to trust Him to guide us rather than think we can plan out the future without His help. I didn't know exactly what the future held for Abby, but I knew I could trust God with taking the first step and doing what I knew was best for her at that moment.

The heart of man plans his way, but the Lord establishes his steps.

— Proverbs 16:9

Big Picture, Small Details

For parents, participating in evaluations can be tricky. You want to acknowledge that your child has needs so you can receive help to meet those needs. But you also don't want to overemphasize your child's weaknesses and have them labeled or categorized in a negative way. The fact that Down syndrome has a physical and genetic diagnosis makes a portion of that easier, but there are also times when we would love to avoid any labels being placed on Abby. Anytime there is a label, there is an assumption. People automatically make assumptions about Abby simply because she has Down syndrome. This can make it more difficult to receive accurate evaluations. This is often to Abby's detriment, as people assume that she will be unable to accomplish tasks or achieve goals.

In larger institutions, labels have become quite common in

efforts to streamline programs and make them more efficient. However, in our experience, most labels merely serve to eliminate personal and individual characteristics, and in the end, they reduce the effectiveness of the program. Labels may have some benefit in helping us to understand a particular individual, and a combination of labels or descriptive words can help us communicate information about that person. But the label should never take the place of the individual.

Many parents who have a child with a disability find certain terms offensive for this reason. The label "retarded," though it may accurately describe a certain characteristic or tendency, has become taboo because it has been used too often as a pejorative. Some parents focus a significant amount of attention on the words used to describe their child. For example, they instruct others to use the term "child with Down syndrome" instead of saying "a Down syndrome child." Down syndrome is merely one aspect of who Abby is and not a characteristic that applies to every aspect of her life. Personally, I choose to extend grace to others who may not have been educated about the correct use of terms. I no longer take personal offense to the labels or phrases or terminology that people use, as I once may have done. It's easy to find things that can make me angry, but I find I only harm myself if I allow myself to become angry about every little thing like the words people use. I must consider the big picture of life and focus on the aspects that are most important and avoid becoming mired in the smaller details that so often destroy relationships. I can recognize opportunities to develop relationships and encourage and teach others when I choose to overlook minor details such as whether they use the correct terminology.

As Abby has grown, she has begun to have her own preferences of the terms we use for her. Instead of being called short, Abby likes the terminology of being "fun-sized." Instead of being labeled as someone with special needs, she likes to be called "unique." Rather than using words that might convey a negative message, we can choose to use words that will encourage and inspire. Rather than focusing on the errors that people make with the words they use, we can focus on helping them better understand the individual, including how to use words and labels appropriately to help people connect.

❧ ❧ ❧

> Good sense makes one slow to anger, and it is his glory to overlook an offense.
>
> — Proverbs 19:11

Filling the Toolbox

Not all assessments, evaluations, and labels are harmful. Some evaluation tools use labels in ways that can help us to better define and identify our child's strengths and weaknesses. Our good friend Dr. Kathy Koch has written a book titled 8 Great Smarts,[1] which we found very helpful with all of our kids. This book was one of the tools that helped us to identify which strengths or "smarts" were more prevalent in each child and which ones needed further development. In the book, Dr. Kathy provides practical application of how to use these labels, or "smarts," for individual application. For example, we learned that Abby is naturally "people smart," and we can share this understanding with others by using this label.

The 5 Love Languages[2] by Gary Chapman is another book that presents a set of labels that were useful to help us identify how each member of our family naturally gives and receives love. As we identify these natural tendencies in ourselves and others, we can learn to demonstrate love to each other in ways that are more readily received, and we can learn to receive love in ways that we may not have previously recognized.

John Trent created another tool that can be helpful for a quick

49

personality evaluation.[3] We have enjoyed identifying each family member's natural tendencies in whether they are more like a lion, otter, beaver, or golden retriever. When we all begin to recognize certain character traits that are more prevalent in each individual, we gain a better understanding of how to relate to each other in more effective ways.

When we use these tools in combination to describe Abby, we can better understand how she is naturally people smart, with a primary love language of quality time, and a personality that is loyal like a golden retriever. We can then help her utilize her natural gifts more effectively to minister to others, help her develop other character qualities that don't come as naturally, better love her by spending quality time with her, and recognize the loyalty and devotion that she exhibits through her golden retriever type personality.

These are just a few examples of how labels can be helpful. Even the label "retarded" can help provide an accurate description of one characteristic of an individual. The difference is in how the tools are used. When used to draw us together, to help us connect and better understand each other, these labels are good and appropriate. If used to separate, segregate, or denigrate, they can cause significant harm.

In our culture today, labels have become a pretty big deal. Labels can be seen almost every day in news reports, and they are often used to separate us according to various sexual identities or orientations or according to our various races, ethnicities, cultures, or beliefs. Unfortunately, some media outlets and organizations choose to use labels to purposely divide us and encourage us to criticize and oppose and even cause harm to those who have labels different than our own. Certain labels are almost always used to divide and separate, and they seldom serve to draw us together. Other labels are most often used to draw us together. We must use the tools at our disposal with wisdom and care.

The way we, as a society, choose to label and either segregate or include people with disabilities is an indication of how we function as a whole. Our relationship (both as a society and as an individual) with those who have special needs is a foundational relationship that determines and defines how we will treat others. If we separate ourselves from those who are "different" and believe ourselves to be superior or more valuable than those with Down syndrome, we will likely also think of ourselves as superior or more valuable than individuals that we define with other labels. But when we include people with Down syndrome and view them as valuable members of our groups, as being equally worthy of our time and resources, then we will most likely also see those with other labels through that same set of values. Abby's brothers are often praised by others for their maturity, and I believe this maturity has developed in large part from their understanding that Abby has equal value and from recognizing that everyone else around them is valuable as well.

God defines us as humans in certain ways that are important for us to recognize. One label God uses for us is "sheep." Sheep wander off into danger. They are believed to be some of the most ignorant of all animals. God also says that we are like little children. We are told to have faith like a child. When we choose to be adopted into His family, we become children of the King of Kings and have an inheritance waiting for us that is beyond anything we can imagine. God also tells us that we are made in His image. We are creative as He is creative. We are eternal as He is eternal. We can use God's labels to define ourselves more accurately as wandering sheep, as children who have much to learn yet are highly valued and protected and created in His image. When we understand how to label ourselves correctly, we will inevitably change our behavior to match that understanding.

 Do nothing from selfish ambition or conceit, but in humility count others more significant than yourselves. Let each of you look not only to his own interests, but also to the interests of others.

— Philippians 2: 3–4

"I myself will be the shepherd of my sheep, and I myself will make them lie down," declares the LORD GOD. "I will seek the lost, and I will bring back the strayed, and I will bind up the injured, and I will strengthen the weak, and the fat and the strong I will destroy. I will feed them in justice."

— Ezekiel 34:15-16

All we like sheep have gone astray; We have turned - every one - to his own way; and the LORD has laid on him the iniquity of us all.

— Isaiah 53:6

See what kind of love the Father has given to us, that we should be called children of God; and so we are.

— 1 John 3:1

Blessed be the God and Father of our Lord Jesus Christ! According to his great mercy, he has caused us to be born again to a living hope through the resurrection of Jesus Christ from the dead, to an inheritance that is imperishable, undefiled, and unfading, kept in heaven for you, who by God's power are being guarded through faith for a salvation ready to be revealed in the last time.

— 1 Peter 1: 3–5

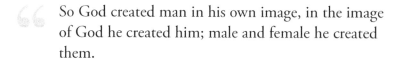 So God created man in his own image, in the image of God he created him; male and female he created them.

— Genesis 1:27

 For Further Reflection

- Do you believe your role as a parent is important? Why or why not?
- Can you identify lies you have believed that keep you from enjoying time with your children?
- Thinking back to caregivers you had when you were a child, can you identify ways that they demonstrated understanding of your needs and ways they helped you reach your potential?
- Did your parents address your needs adequately when you were a child, or did you rely more on teachers or others?
- Do you agree that the responsibility for caring for children is given to parents?
- Can you identify places in the Bible where God addresses who is responsible for teaching children?
- How much emphasis do you place on outward appearance? Does your opinion of others change based on how they look?
- Do you understand that God's love for you does not depend on how you look on the outside?
- Do you feel you need to have the end goal and every step planned before beginning an endeavor, or are you able to start a new venture without knowing where you're going or how you'll get there? Do you trust God with each step?
- What are some of the labels that have been used to describe you or your child? How do you respond to those labels?

- How do you use labels? Do you use them to draw people together or separate them?
- How do the labels that God uses for us in the Bible change the way you think about yourself or others?

Chapter 3

Conform or Transform: Setting and Maintaining Standards

 Do not be conformed to this world, but be transformed by the renewal of your mind, that by testing you may discern what is the will of God, what is good and acceptable and perfect.

— Romans 12:2

Each time we interact with someone new, we are influenced by a different set of beliefs and values. Whether we recognize it or not, people impact our thinking. With each new interaction, we have a decision to make. We must test and "discern what is the will of God." With each experience, we must decide: Will we be influenced by others and choose to conform to someone else's standard? Or will we influence others by how we have already been transformed? When we are first transformed by God, we can then have confidence to stand firm in our convictions. Rather than conforming to outside influences, we can instead transform the world around us.

Our role as Abby's parents has provided unique opportunities for us to demonstrate to others how we have been transformed by God. As we continue to gain a better understanding of God's standard for our lives, and the more we chose to adhere to that standard, the more confidently we are then able to maintain that standard. While we have clearly struggled in our attempts to adhere to God's standard, and we have not always been successful in demonstrating it clearly to others, we have attempted to obey the command of this verse in Romans 12 in our interaction with friends, neighbors, teachers, and even strangers. I pray this section will help you to consider how your relationships and your adherence to God's standard can help you to be transformed and become more like God.

Environments and Friendships: Belonging

A popular television show in the '80s and early '90s had a theme song that stated, "Sometimes you want to go where everybody knows your name." Don't we all enjoy being around others who know us well and share common interests? As we consider the labels we use, we can also consider the various ways they can help us connect to others who share the same values or interests. Among those who have disabilities, some choose to focus on the label that draws them to other individuals with similar disabilities. There can be solace and comfort in finding those who are like you, who share the same struggles.

We have developed strong friendships with several families who also have a child with Down syndrome that is close in age with Abby. These friends are dear to us and have been such a help to us through the years. We share resources, we strengthen each other, and we confide in each other when we experience difficulties. It is a blessing to find people who understand what you are going through because they may have gone through it themselves or can at least empathize better than others because of their similar experiences or characteristics.

What we realized early on, though, is that it isn't healthy for us to remain secluded with these friends. While we find encouragement from them, it would not be best for us to have only friendships with other families that have a child with Down syndrome.

When Abby was one and a half years old, we enrolled her in a school specifically for kids with Down syndrome called The Rise School.[1]

It was a full-time program that included integrated therapies and targeted instruction to help very young children with Down syndrome overcome the struggles that were common among them. The program was a wonderful help to our family, and we learned a lot through our participation there. It was a struggle for me to leave Abby at school full-time at eighteen months of age. I spent as much time there with her at the school as possible, and I learned all I could about the therapies they were using. After the first two weeks, I told the school director how much difficulty I was having being separated from Abby. It didn't seem right to me to spend so much time away from her and delegate her care to others at such a young age. I asked if we could switch Abby's schedule to part- time attendance, and the director agreed to accommodate my desires.

Over the course of the year, we continued to reduce the amount of time Abby spent at the school. By the end of the school year, she was attending only two mornings each week.

I learned a lot during the time we spent at The Rise School. I learned about new therapies and how to better integrate a variety of therapies into our daily activities. I also learned that Abby had a strong tendency to mimic the behaviors of other children around her. I recalled that when Abby was first born, someone recommended that we have another child right away so she would have a sibling to model typical behaviors as they grew up together. I could see that Abby intently watched her older brother.

Unfortunately, we found that she also mimicked negative oral motor habits of other kids with Down syndrome. During her time at The Rise School, Abby developed a significant habit of forward tongue protrusion, a challenge that is very common among kids with Down syndrome. It was something Abby had not really struggled with before attending the school, but it became a huge obstacle for us to overcome. We would spend many hours of oral motor therapy dedicated to helping her control her tongue.

Because of this experience, we recognized early in Abby's life that it was important for her to spend time around peers who would exhibit appropriate behaviors. Our friends with Down syndrome have wonderful character qualities and are beautiful people that we enjoy spending time with. But some physical struggles can become magnified when you spend time only around others who share that same struggle.

We recognized early in Abby's life that it was important for her to spend time around peers who would exhibit appropriate behaviors.

When we are striving to overcome a challenge, we can learn from those who are successful in their efforts to overcome, and it is usually unwise to spend all our time with those who share the same struggle and allow that struggle to define us.

It can be tempting to focus on the struggle and define yourself as a victim, and to desire to be around others who receive, understand, and share your complaints. I have not seen this pattern of behavior to be productive, so I chose to avoid spending much time around others who stayed in this mindset.

We saw Abby mimic positive behaviors in her older brother, and we desired for her to have more peers who would be a positive influence on her. Thankfully, God has brought some beautiful people into our lives who have become good friends to Abby. We have observed how Abby provides an opportunity for others to display the genuine kindness that God has grown in their hearts. It is not only a blessing for Abby, but also for everyone else around her. What has been especially fun to see is those times when one young woman embraces Abby as a friend and others are encouraged to see Abby as a friend as well. The actions of one person who accepts and embraces Abby can influence a whole community.

Rather than separating those with unique needs and allowing them to congregate together, I see great benefit in the idea of integration and the many positive results of having people with unique needs included in our groups.

> In the same way, let your light shine before others, so that they may see your good works and give glory to your Father who is in heaven.
>
> — Matthew 5:16

Reducing Restrictions

When Abby first qualified to receive special services in our local public school at age three, I assumed there would be a place for her in an inclusive environment with peers who would model good behavior. Because I was convinced that this was best not only for Abby but for other students as well, I was very disappointed when they did not provide this kind of environment. For several months, I met with school administrators and studied laws that specified what the government school was required to provide. The law required the school to provide the "least restrictive environment" for the child. I learned about schools in other states that were implementing inclusive practices successfully.

Students with Down syndrome were being educated in regular classrooms with typical-developing peers, and therapy was integrated in the classroom so that all students could benefit and so that individual students would not have to be removed from the classroom in order to receive the specific help they needed. This practice of inclusion was happening in other schools with great success, and I knew this model of education was the least restrictive environment for Abby.

I presented these facts and examples in meeting after meeting, and I requested that administrators consider how they could provide a similar learning environment for Abby and others like her. I enlisted advocacy organizations to assist me and even met with individual members of the school board. At least one school board member and a few of the school employees were receptive to our requests, and we were asked to consider serving on the school board in order to work towards implementing new policies and methods like what we were suggesting. We debated about whether our involvement there could make a difference in the school system.

We ultimately decided that the government school system was already too broken and that our time and efforts would be more effective and productive if focused on other environments, and particularly on our own children. In the many meetings with school personnel that we had already attended, we discovered that our single vote did not produce any change when several others voted to direct funding elsewhere.

We knew Abby had the ability to be in a regular classroom with typical-developing kids, which was the least restrictive environment for her and was required by law. We did make some progress when an advocacy organization came to represent us and essentially forced school administrators to place Abby in a regular classroom. Unfortunately, the only regular classroom they were willing to consider was their pre-K class that consisted of students who were at least one if not two years older than Abby, and most were students in the ESL program (English as a Second Language). We reluctantly agreed to give this a try, though some of the students were twice as big as Abby, and we had some concerns about her safety and language development. Teachers were clearly surprised at how well Abby functioned among these typical-developing students. We wanted Abby to fully participate in classroom activities, and she was clearly able to do so. As time passed, however, we recognized reasons why this particular classroom environment was not safe for Abby.

Abby had the ability to play on playground equipment that was appropriate for her size, but the jungle gym that the five-year-old boys played on was dangerous for a petite three-year-old girl with Down syndrome. Abby tried to climb right along with the big boys, but she needed constant supervision on that particular playground equipment. Rather than following Abby around the playground, the teachers told Abby she couldn't do the same activities the other kids were doing. As I observed this scenario one day, I recognized how harmful it was for Abby to be told that she could not do what the other kids were doing. She didn't know that the reason she couldn't do it was because she did not have adequate help and supervision or appropriately sized equipment on which to play.

We wanted Abby to try everything she could, to be allowed to do as much as she was able, to be told she could rather than told she couldn't. I would not allow others to tell her she couldn't do things simply because they wouldn't even let her try. Abby needed to be in an environment where she could take appropriate risks and push herself to achieve to her full capability. The public-school administrators were either unable or unwilling to provide such an environment, in spite of our repeated requests that they consider other options that we knew were better and more appropriate. Rather than choosing to conform to a lower standard of care for Abby, we continued to hold onto a better standard and seek out an environment where she could take appropriate risks and challenges.

Taking Appropriate Risks

Our family has spent many hours walking to our neighborhood parks. When the kids were little, we lived near what we called the yellow park and the white park. It was a great blessing to live in a neighborhood with walking paths and playground areas that had equipment for all ages.

As is the case with most kids, Abby wanted to do all the things she saw her older brother doing. We taught Caleb that it was important for him to provide a good example for her, and because he loved his little sister, he chose to be that positive example that she needed. Caleb loved being adventurous and exploring all his capabilities on the playground. Abby tried to keep up. The yellow park included a wonderful tunnel slide.

Abby saw her older brother slide through that tunnel, and of course, she wanted to try it for herself. She was so tiny, and that slide seemed so big in comparison. We have a photo of Abby going down that slide with her eyes closed, fully trusting that her dad was there to catch her. She was able to take the risk and fully enjoy that tunnel slide with a huge smile on her face because she knew her family was there to ensure that she would be safe.

Abby was willing to attempt many activities because we believed in her and encouraged her to try. She has been successful in water-skiing, speech competitions, and playing basketball and cheer-leading and soccer through community sports programs such as Upward.[2] She had confidence knowing that her family was cheering for her to do well. She was willing to try all those activities because she had a relationship of trust with us. We encouraged her to take the risks that were necessary to explore these activities, and then we supported her when she tried, even if she had difficulty. We often "bribed" Abby with the promise of her favorite meal in order to help motivate her to keep trying until she was successful. This technique was often effective, especially when motivating her to water-ski! She was so proud and excited about her progress when she would finally achieve the goal and knew the reward that would come.

Abby was willing to attempt many activities because we believed in her and encouraged her to try.

Tyce and I often encouraged our kids to take risks in activities that we knew would be good for them. We challenged them with horseback riding and sailing and encouraged them to engage in various activities that would push them to the extent of their abilities. We tried to always be aware of their ability level so that we didn't push too hard or cause them to become overly frustrated. For example, we encouraged Abby to try driving and provided opportunities for her to do so. But when she began to recognize her difficulty in responding quickly to situations that would arise, we did not continue to push her to a point of being overly fearful or frustrated.

We also tried to avoid anything that might encourage our kids to venture into activities that we knew would be harmful. As our kids grew older and as they were ready, we explained to them some of the harmful experiences we had when we were younger and how we wanted to help them avoid dealing with the negative effects of similar harmful influences. Movies and music are some of the most common influences that can present ongoing harm to our kids. We've been thankful for short clips of movies that are available to us now on the internet that allow us to share some of the fun parts of what we've experienced without having to wade through all the negative parts as well. We've never understood the philosophy of exposing kids to things that are known to be harmful in order to help them learn how to respond.

As we've observed other parents allowing or even encouraging their kids to take risks and be exposed to things that we believed were clearly harmful, we struggled to understand the rationale. I've heard the reasoning that kids need to learn to be tough, but it seems to me that life is hard enough without having to purposely add more difficulty to it. When parents purposely, or at least knowingly, expose their kids to harmful situations and influences, the child may begin to develop a mindset of distrust towards their parents. If the child eventually recognizes the harm, they may begin to believe that their parents did not truly care for them. Lack of trust in the relationship may be the result.

We wanted our kids to continue to trust us. We tried to avoid anything that would erode their trust in us, and as a result, we avoided even some of the most popular things in our culture, including things like Santa Claus and the Easter Bunny. We taught our kids what we knew to be true about Saint Nicholas, and we decided together that we could enjoy pretending, but they knew all along what was real and what was pretend. We noticed how important it was for our kids to learn things right the first time whenever possible. So much of our own lives had been spent unlearning and relearning, we wanted our kids to have the benefit of hearing the truth and learning things correctly from the beginning, at least as far as it was possible for us to do.

With Abby, it was even more important to learn things right the first time. We learned to rethink everything because of Abby having Down syndrome. Down syndrome was the initial reason that we began to question everything. We reevaluated every aspect of life, largely because we couldn't simply conform to the norm or go along with what everyone else was doing. As we began to reevaluate everything, we questioned the core and foundation of education, even asking something as basic as why we educate our kids at all.

We came to recognize that if their education was not focused on glorifying God, it was all in vain. We believed the Bible when it stated that the fear of the LORD is the beginning of wisdom and knowledge. Our kids would not learn anything worthwhile until they had first learned the fear of the LORD.

A friend once asked Tyce, "What is the purpose for teaching your child to read?" Tyce responded with a fairly typical answer about getting a job and providing financially for your family. The man encouraged Tyce to rethink his answer and consider the truth that the best reason to teach our kids to read is so that they can read God's Word. That man was right! What a blessing to have others who came alongside us to help us examine and evaluate the real purpose behind what we were doing with our kids.

Fathers, do not provoke your children to anger, but bring them up in the discipline and instruction of the Lord.

— Ephesians 6:4

The fear of the Lord is the beginning of knowledge; fools despise wisdom and instruction.

— Proverbs 1:7

The fear of the Lord is the beginning of wisdom, and the knowledge of the Holy One is insight.

— Proverbs 9:10

The Search for An Appropriate Education

Many families have had opportunity to reevaluate their lives as a result of recent changes in our society. I've heard it described as a "paradigm shift" or others speak of "deconstructing" even the most foundational truths upon which they established their faith and beliefs. Most of us have questioned everything from education to healthcare to church attendance to even the most fundamental aspects of marriage and gender. Every institution and foundational tenet of our society has been questioned. It is important that our questions lead us to truth rather than the elimination of truth. It is important for us and for our children to know that truth exists, to help them recognize what is true, and to help them make decisions that align with what we know to be true. Questions without answers merely cause frustration and hopelessness. It is our responsibility to help our kids avoid the frustration that can come from too many unanswered questions. We must answer to the best of our ability and lead them to discover truth even when we don't immediately know the answers they seek to find. They need to learn alongside us and see that we are continuing to learn ourselves. One of the blessings of educating our kids at home is that we have all discovered a renewed love for learning. Because God is full of endless truth, I believe we will enjoy learning new things through all of eternity!

It is our responsibility to help our kids avoid the frustration that can come from too many unanswered questions.

As we questioned the public education system and continued to evaluate our purpose for placing Abby in the public-school classroom, we recognized other issues beyond the inappropriate equipment on the playground. One such example is that classroom time was used to show movies that I believed were inappropriate. We came to recognize that when the law requires the school to provide an "appropriate education," it is using a term that is subject to interpretation. As our efforts in the public school failed to provide the education that we knew was best for Abby, we began to explore other options outside the government system.

The final incident that led us to remove Abby from public school happened one day when I arrived a bit early to pick her up. I went into the classroom and observed the last few minutes of class. An aide had pulled Abby to the side of the classroom to work with her separately. After they finished an activity, the aide asked Abby if her diaper was wet. Children with Down syndrome often have difficulty with potty training, and Abby was still unable to recognize when she had wet her diaper. Abby didn't answer the aide's question, so the aide proceeded to thrust her bare hand into Abby's diaper to check. She then proceeded to scold Abby loudly for wetting her diaper, in front of her classmates.

I immediately saw the harm this was doing to Abby and intervened and took Abby home. When I later questioned the extent of training that the aide had received, the administrators told me that she was considered "highly qualified." I asked what that meant specifically, and they told me that it meant she had attended a two-day course on all things related to working with kids with special needs. Tyce and I had learned that Abby needed an extra measure of grace and compassion and patience in potty training due to her physical limitations. The aide clearly had not been trained how to respond appropriately in such situations, though she was considered highly qualified by the schools to work with children with special needs.

It was during a meeting with the school superintendent that I finally came to recognize how the schools were a reflection of the community. The superintendent stated his belief that our community valued football and other sports programs much more than they valued educational programs for kids with special needs. Because of his belief, he made it clear that funding would continue to be directed to those other programs and would not be allocated to providing a better learning environment for kids like Abby. It was our own ignorance of the current state of our public schools that was creating the conflict. When we recognized the difference between what we had expected or hoped for and the reality of how things actually were, we began to see why the inclusive environment we desired for Abby would not happen in our local public schools.

Tyce recognized this much sooner than I did, and he was relieved when I finally decided to stop fighting the school and move in a different direction. This time period in our lives was very difficult, and this conflict had created a lot of strain on our marriage. I found myself feeling continually angry at those who had been tasked with and paid to (through our tax dollars) help us care for our daughter but instead seemed to be harming her. It was unhealthy for all of us to continue in this situation. We did not intend to live our lives as victims who were at the mercy of others. We both finally recognized that our whole family would benefit, and our kids would receive better instruction, if we spent even half the time that we had previously spent fighting the school instead focusing on our kids.

We left the public school and found a Christian preschool right down the road that was a wonderful fit for Abby. Abby was able to fully participate in all activities there with great success. This was the environment that we had been hoping the public school would provide. For a brief time, we felt accepted.

I have written journal entries throughout the years when our kids were growing and changing so rapidly. One entry from this time period, dated November 13, states: "One little girl's (Eme's) mom said that Eme described her class as 'Abby and the other kids.'

Several moms from the nursery at church have said similar things – that Abby is their daughter or son's favorite or that Abby's name was the first word they said. One girl at Abby's school, on Wednesday when I picked up Abby, asked, 'Whose mom is that?' When told, 'That's Abby's mom,' she said, 'I LOVE Abby!'"

Abby soon aged out of the preschool program, and our search for an appropriate classroom began again. We began trying to work with a private Christian school close to our home. We hoped that the values there would produce a different result than what we had found in the public school. While the Christian school administrators demonstrated a clear desire to help us meet Abby's needs and include her in their program, their emphasis on excellence and college preparation made this a challenge as well. We felt acceptance from administrators, they valued Abby and wanted her there, but the knowledge and understanding of how to include Abby was still a missing factor. The private school had not yet explored ways to offer services that would meet Abby's unique needs.

As we began this process of exploration together, it became clear that not everyone at the school was in favor of including children with disabilities in the program. We didn't want to be the cause of division among the families at the school, and we saw that it would be an ongoing challenge to attempt to steer an established school in a new direction. Abby was still in preschool, but Tyce and I were already tired of fighting for acceptance.

It began to feel like no one wanted Abby in their classroom or had the willingness to work with her to help us, even when it was their job to do so. As Abby grew older, she gradually moved further away from her peers and soon did not fit into the typical categories. Because our church followed the public-school model of separating kids by age, we began to encounter the same issues there as well. These systems and methods did not easily accommodate a child like Abby who didn't fit neatly into those categories of separation.

After many attempts to have Abby in inclusive environments with typical developing kids, we learned to quickly move on from those that wouldn't accept her to keep searching for the people who would embrace her and who wanted her. We had nearly resigned ourselves to the fact that there were no such groups, but we kept asking, with the humble recognition that it was unlikely.

A good friend of mine, Geri Green, recently shared this story with me about a time her daughter moved to a new school and tried to fit in to the new environment: "When Emily was in middle school, a school she had recently transferred to, I attended a parent-teacher conference and was told about a time she made the lunch staff laugh out loud. The school lunchroom was always chaotic, I was told, with kids constantly coming in, sitting down, standing up, going out, asking for help, talking amongst themselves, shouting across the tables at one another, etc. It always seemed to bother Emily, as if it was just too much for her to process, but she always sat quietly and ate her lunch, just looking around at all the action. One day, in the middle of all the noise and bustle, Emily stood up and started singing (at the top of her lungs), 'Won't you take me to…

…Funky Town!' Several students and staff members recognized the song because it had recently been featured in an Alvin and the Chipmunks movie. Some sang along, some danced, and some laughed. The principal decided Funky Town should become the official lunchroom song because it was the perfect description of their cafeteria."

Finding Where We Fit

Though we had nearly given up in our attempts to find an environment where Abby could easily be included, we kept pressing forward. As the next summer began, our older son attended camp at a place that is about as close to heaven on earth as I've found. It's a camp called Pine Cove.

When we picked up Caleb at the end of camp, we observed how much fun he had and the spiritual growth that had happened in him during his week there. Tyce approached one of the directors, pointed to Abby, and made the comment, "We sure would like our daughter to be able to come to camp here. I don't suppose there's any possibility of Abby attending?" The director immediately responded by expressing the desire of the camp leaders to have kids like Abby there, and he said they had been praying about this as leaders of the camp. It was so beautiful to find a group of people who saw value in having Abby in their program and who recognized the lessons that could be learned from her participation! This camp was a rare place where we did not have to fight to advocate for our daughter, because they welcomed her and embraced her and saw her value. They worked with us to do anything that was necessary for her to be included to the full extent possible.

Abby was able to attend camp there every year for the next ten years. She was able to participate fully alongside typical developing peers. It was a tremendous learning experience, not only for Abby but also for the other campers, counselors, and others at the camp. Abby learned to develop independence, gain confidence, be bold in sharing with others, function on a team. She developed wonderful friendships. Each year when we would bring Abby back to camp, people would recognize her and welcome her warmly. It was a place where Abby knew she was welcomed and accepted, loved and valued.

We don't really know the full extent to which the camp worked to accommodate Abby. We know that the first year Abby attended, they dedicated one counselor to spend the whole week with Abby, coming alongside her to ensure that everything went smoothly. Soon they realized that Abby did not need her own counselor. We are thankful that they made the initial investment so that Abby could gradually demonstrate her abilities and be successful there.

We longed to find this same acceptance for Abby in other environments. After our attempts to include Abby in both public and private full-time classrooms, we decided to try homeschooling.

Thankfully, we have found parents in homeschooling communities to be more accepting and welcoming. In university-model schools, we found the ability to place Abby into the classroom that best fit her learning level. She was often able to be included without the same stigma that we faced in full-time schools. In home-schooling groups, we found fewer labels, wider variety in each classroom, more openness, and a much greater likelihood that others would value Abby as a child of God, as someone who had inherent value and worth, as someone they wanted to know as a friend. What a blessing it was to develop these friendships! As Abby has grown, God has always provided what she needed for friendship and companionship. She's not been wildly popular, by any means, but she has some really good friends.

Overcoming Isolation – and Gifts for Abby

We recognize now that even when Abby didn't have many friends in her life, God was providing what she needed. The year we decided to graduate Abby out of school was the same year that her big brother left for college. It was also the same year that her two best friends moved out of state.

Abby felt very lonely. She struggled to engage with new friends in new environments, but she turned to God for comfort and found the strength she needed. God directed her through these times and helped her gain understanding that would provide peace and contentment for her, in spite of not having many friends. It was not the first time we had experienced loneliness and not the first time that we found God to be our continual and consistent companion who was sufficient to meet all our needs.

It was not the first time we had experienced loneliness and not the first time that we found God to be our continual and consistent companion who was sufficient to meet all our needs.

When Abby was only about two months old, she caught a cold. It was the middle of winter, and we had just begun to venture out into the world with our fragile newborn after many weeks of being on bedrest and then adjusting to being a family of four. Abby's cold did not go away, and she began to have difficulty breathing, so I took her back to our pediatrician. I assumed he would give us a prescription to help her get better, and life would soon settle back into our new normal. Next thing I knew, the doctor was writing four different prescriptions and giving me instructions for how to operate a nebulizer and administer medicine to Abby every four hours, night and day. He explained that she had RSV, Respiratory Syncytial Virus, and that treatment would likely be needed for four to six months. All my hopes of venturing out again and returning to "normal" life suddenly vanished. After leaving the doctor's office, I sat in the car and cried.

I know now that RSV is a common virus, and we are certainly not alone in having this experience. But at the time, I had no idea how serious the complications of this virus could be. As I look at information about RSV now, I see that Abby possessed all the risk factors for this virus to potentially cause significant harm. Thankfully, I knew enough at the time to follow the doctor's orders. We fought RSV for many months, and honestly, it seemed that Abby never fully recovered. She struggled with respiratory issues for many years, and eventually, she was diagnosed with asthma, which may have been caused by the RSV. It seemed that every time we took

Abby to church, she would catch another cold that would turn into an infection or bigger problem. We got to the point where, when we walked into the children's area at church and saw a child with a runny nose, we would immediately decide to turn around and go back home.

What was a minor cold for a few days for one child would be a month- long event, a doctor's office visit, and another round of antibiotics for Abby. This pattern repeated month after month, and we began to feel very isolated and lonely. Primarily for this reason, we moved to a smaller church with fewer children, one that was closer to our home, in hopes that we could again develop friendships and re-engage in worship with a church congregation.

In those days when we were cooped up at home and I was administering breathing treatments every four hours, I began to sing to Abby more regularly. As I would sing songs to her, I thought about how she would receive the words. She was just beginning to understand the world, and many of the common children's songs had no meaning to her. Some of the older ones can be downright scary for a small child! I mean, one talks of a cradle in a treetop, and the song ends with: "Down will come baby, cradle and all." I began to recognize even more just how important it was to choose appropriate content for my children in everything they hear and see.

More broadly, during those moments of helping Abby breathe, everything else seemed to fade away. Because I had to physically hold the tube close to her face, there was little else we could do but talk or sing or rest. No matter what other tasks were on my list, in those moments she had my full attention. As I spent that time with her, my love for her grew deeper. I thought about what she really needed; I considered what her future might be like; I dreamed about the kind of person she might become. I soon ran out of songs to sing to her that had words I wanted her to remember. I began to make up words and melodies with messages I wanted her to always remember.

Two of the songs I wrote during this time became her favorites.

I recently recorded them so that she will always have them and in hopes that other parents might enjoy singing them to their kids as well. One song tells a story of a little girl who wants to be a princess. Abby loved to dress up and pretend she was a princess. I wanted Abby to know she could be a princess, a daughter of the King of Kings. No matter who else was in her life, God would always be there with her and He always loves her. I was reminded myself that God is always with me and loves me as well. Perhaps you can sing them to a little girl in your life who wants to be a princess. (Links to these songs can be found at the end of this book.)

In hopes of sharing this message with others, I've also published one of the stories I often told Abby about a girl wanting to become a princess. It's titled *Becoming Beautiful Princess Prisca*,[3] and can be found at the end of this section of the book. It is filled with Scripture to help young girls learn about becoming a daughter of the King of Kings.

Guarding Her Heart

Abby was captivated by Disney princess movies. As she tells it now, she idolized Disney princesses. It wasn't until she was about sixteen or seventeen years old that she finally recognized how her view of Disney princesses was harmful.

Tyce and I knew that much of the emphasis of Disney movies was selfish and harmful. However, among our friends, we had difficulty explaining why we would not allow her to watch certain movies. We gave in and allowed her to watch several of the most popular or older stories that we had seen when we were kids. While we may have seen the movie once or twice as a child, Abby was able to watch the movies over and over on videos. The messages became ingrained in her thinking, and she began to exhibit selfish attitudes and behaviors. When we addressed these attitudes and helped her recognize the reality of how they were influencing her and how the messages she was receiving were contrary to God's Word, she responded with a contrite heart. She now loves to share her testimony of how she chose to put aside the Disney princess idols and give God the place of highest honor in her life.

Tyce, of course, helped many times with breathing treatments He often sang hymns with Abby as he administered the medication through the nebulizer. His relationship with Abby became a sweet and beautiful expression of the tender love of a caring father for his daughter. They developed a special bond. Abby came to trust Tyce completely and still looks to him first for advice. If Tyce and I ever disagree, I know she will most likely take his side!

When Abby had heart surgery, I was nursing our newborn, Luke, and could not take him into the ICU. Tyce took on much of the responsibility to be by Abby's side as she recovered from surgery. Their bond was strengthened through that experience, as Abby came to trust him even more to be there for her when she was hurting.

As our kids grew older, we attended several homeschool conventions together as a family. At first, we were quite overwhelmed with the options available there. Soon enough, we all became more comfortable and confident in navigating the options and finding resources that served well to fit our needs. Abby engaged as well and chose books that were of interest to her. One such book that she presented to Tyce and asked him to read with her is titled The Three Weavers.[4]

As Tyce and Abby read this book and prayed together, God helped Abby find peace and become more content and discerning in her relationships. We have been continually amazed at how God provides just the right resource to meet our needs when we pray and trust Him to lead.

Where Abby previously had been "boy-crazy" and focused on finding her Prince Charming, God now helped her find peace in the fact that she might never be married. Abby learned that God was all she needed, and she has found contentment in being single.

Many times, we have recognized a need, prayed about it, then would soon find that God already had an answer waiting. As we prayed, He opened our eyes to see what was there all along and directed us how to find it.

Before they call I will answer; while they are yet speaking I will hear.

— Isaiah 65:24

 For Further Reflection

- Do you find yourself spending time mostly with others who share the same struggles?
- Are these relationships healthy or do they allow you to remain in unhealthy habits?
- How can you encourage your children to take appropriate risks and challenge them to achieve their full capabilities?
- What factors prevent you from encouraging your kids to take appropriate risks or embrace new challenges?
- Do you provide your child with the security they need to risk trying new things? Do they know that you will be there to catch them if they fall?
- Who are the positive role models that your children have in their lives to mimic?
- Do you allow your child to take inappropriate risks that you know will be harmful to them?
- Have your children developed inappropriate attitudes resulting from media they have been allowed to consume?
- Do you believe that the fear of the LORD is the beginning of wisdom and knowledge? Have you taught your children what it means to fear the LORD?
- Do your children have many unanswered questions that cause them to be frustrated or feel hopeless?
- Have you and your child both developed a love for learning? Do your children observe that you continue to learn as an adult? Is it important to you to continue to learn?

- Do you enjoy learning about God and exploring the vastness of who He is and all He has created?

Chapter 4

Inward Adjustments

Marriage Matters

Tyce and I recognize that during the years when we felt so isolated and lonely, we grew closer together as a couple and as a family. Just as the times of isolation with Abby while administering breathing treatments helped us develop a deeper love for her, the times of isolation from friends helped Tyce and I depend on each other and love each other more deeply as well. God used our struggles with Abby's health and education to strengthen our marriage. God helped us see that we needed each other and that we needed to work together as a team.

We had many arguments along the way, and we jokingly said that Tyce needed a T-shirt with a big target on it because so often he became the target upon which I released my frustration. It was at a FamilyLife Weekend to Remember[1] that I began to recognize what I was doing and how harmful it was for me to blame him for so many difficulties.

When we were first married, I thought having a husband would solve many of my problems and meet many of my needs. It took a while to realize that my expectations were wrong. I gradually learned that my husband was not the one I should trust to provide everything I needed. My husband was not the one I should expect to make everything right or solve every problem. My husband was not even the one who I should expect to make me happy. I learned that marriage is not about my happiness. Because we were forced to work together to meet Abby's needs, because we had so few friends to turn to for comfort, because we had so little time to connect with others outside our family but so much time at home with our kids, we learned to depend on each other and work through the difficulties together.

Now I look back on those times of difficulty and I'm thankful for what God did in our marriage and in our family and how He sustained us and helped us develop a much deeper love for each other through what we once saw as difficulty and suffering. We developed a regular habit of going on walks together that has become a sustaining and important time we share together. Our walks are a necessary conduit for communicating with each other, but they also serve to provide the real intimacy and companionship that meet our deepest desires.

> This mystery is profound, and I am saying that it
> refers to Christ and the church. However, let each one
> of you love his wife as himself, and let the wife see
> that she respects her husband.

— Ephesians 5:32-33

Self Care | Balance | Asking for Help

When my kids were little and my life was consumed with caring for them, it seemed that my desires were at the bottom of the list of priorities for a very long time. I didn't find anyone telling me to make sure I take care of myself, though I sought out that advice and longed for someone to give it. Self-care is a topic that has become important to many women in recent years. When I see the term "self-care," I think of the blogs I've read about moms who want to escape with a glass of wine, a hot bath, their favorite candle and some chocolates. Or perhaps they want to spend a weekend binge-watching their favorite show. While I certainly enjoy chocolate and a nice bubble bath now and then, I've never found these kinds of activities able to fulfill my need for real renewal and encouragement. Simply attempting to escape my reality does little to help and can often even leave me worse than before. If I spend too much time watching television or escaping my reality, I return to find the reality that my list of tasks to accomplish just seems bigger and I feel yucky. A short escape may provide some rest when I'm really weary, but it often still leaves me feeling empty.

Simply attempting to escape my reality does little to help and can often even leave me worse than before.

During the time of life when my kids were young and required constant attention, I did need breaks now and then. Sometimes I simply needed a nap. But beyond physical rest, I also needed to be encouraged and strengthened and built up emotionally and mentally. I would often see advertisements for mom's retreat weekends, but I didn't think it was possible to take a whole weekend away. I tend to think of myself as irreplaceable, and especially so because of Abby's unique needs. But Tyce and I both recognized that I needed a longer break to renew my spirit. I had to admit that I couldn't do everything on my own. I needed God to renew and strengthen me.

We should not be ashamed to ask for help. Our society is very individualized, and we seldom see extended family helping each other like they once did. I don't know many women who have regular help from family or close friends. Many of us now tackle parenting alone. But when we are extremely weary and really need rest, it is okay to approach someone and ask for help. When we finally find someone that seems capable of caring for our kids in our place, we need to utilize the time they give us wisely.

The key is finding which activities help strengthen and renew your mind and spirit. God made us in His image, and we are creative just as He is creative. I believe that we need to re-create in order to be renewed.

We need to re-create
in order to be renewed.

I mentioned before that I like to write songs. Creating songs while at the piano is an activity that renews my spirit. If you don't already have activities that you know help you feel renewed, I hope you will explore various creative outlets until you find something that really strengthens and renews you. Allow yourself to take time when you need to renew your strength. Don't run on empty, because you will soon putter out! Call on friends who recognize that you need to recreate and who will help you find ways to renew your strength. We should strive to have at least a few friends or family members in our lives who truly want what is best for us and who are willing to sacrifice themselves to help us find what we really need.

I'm so thankful for those people in my life who care for me in this way. Even though my mother has never lived near to me, she has often recognized my need for rest and come to help care for our kids so that I could have time of respite and renewal. I am so thankful for her willingness to sacrifice her time to help provide what I needed.

It is an especially beautiful thing when God provides time through the generous love of a friend or family member and then helps you use the gifts that He gives you to create something that helps someone else.

I was recently told that the best form of self-care is serving others. It seems ironic, doesn't it? But I have found it's true. This advice was a good reminder of how important it is to take my focus off myself, while still using the combination of gifts that God has given uniquely to me, to care for others. It is a special gift when God provides ways for us to shift from caring for our children to caring for others in different ways. Sometimes we can do both at the same time.

When our kids were little, we sought to find ministry that we could do together as a family. We made it a habit to visit residents in local nursing homes, to play card games or sing hymns or take gifts to them. Each time we went, it seemed like a great effort to get everyone out the door and on our way. Tyce and I often felt we didn't really have the strength to do it. But it was amazing how, afterwards, we always felt encouraged and strengthened. Through our giving to those residents out of our own weakness, God somehow strengthened us.

When we recognize in our weakness that everything we have comes from God, that every good gift is from Him, and we surrender ourselves to His plan, using all that we have received to give back to Him and worship Him, He renews us and strengthens us in ways that I struggle to explain with logic and reason. You have likely heard the verse in Acts 20:35 in which Jesus is quoted as saying, "It is more blessed to give than to receive." This verse doesn't seem to make sense if we consider only the ways of the world, but In God's economy and His ways, I have found it to certainly be true.

❧ ❧ ❧

> I thank my God in all my remembrance of you, always in every prayer of mine for you all making my prayer with joy, because of your partnership in the gospel from the first day until now.
>
> — Philippians 1:3-5

> Every good gift and every perfect gift is from above, coming down from the Father of lights, with whom there is no variation or shadow due to change.
>
> — James 1:17

When You Feel Alone

There were times when I did not have help available, when I knew that even my mom was unable to come and help, and I felt that I had completely run out of strength. I remember crying out to God, asking Him why He left me so alone, and then realizing that I was not alone. He was there. He sustained me. He gave the strength I needed when there was no one else to help and I had no strength left of my own.

Shortly after Luke was born, the small church we attended experienced a time of transition. Many of our friends moved to other churches, but we stayed. The church had been such a wonderful support to us during the time of my pregnancy and Abby's heart surgery; we wanted to give back and contribute something to the congregation. I spent my time at church in the nursery with Luke and one or two other babies. Tyce most often spent his time in the elementary classroom, teaching the first through sixth graders. We seldom had an opportunity to worship or attend Bible classes together, and we became very weary. We were committed to the church even though we no longer had the same level of support that we were accustomed to having. I remember one week feeling very discouraged and longing for time worshiping the Lord with other believers. I needed that fellowship and encouragement that comes when we acknowledge together what God has done and how He sustains us, so I attended another church that had an evening worship service. Unfortunately, I didn't find the community and support and strengthening that I was searching for. It was God alone who sustained us through this time. We learned to rely completely on Him. We found that He was always enough to meet our needs.

During this time, a weekend conference for moms again came to my attention. My husband strongly encouraged me to attend and said he would take care of the kids so I could go. I registered and made a purposeful goal of renewing my spirit and focusing on God that weekend. I was amazed at how much I learned about God and about life through taking a step away and making it a priority to focus on Him. I found renewal that was real, and it was worth the time and effort to get away from my responsibilities at home and find that strength from God that I needed. My strength was renewed as I was able to worship with other believers and recognize how God continues to provide.

Come to me, all who labor and are heavy laden, and I will give you rest.

— Matthew 11:28

Learning to Let Go

In order to attend that conference, I had to change my mindset of thinking that I was irreplaceable and instead believe that my husband really could care for the kids on his own! I had to admit that I needed help and that something needed to change. I recall another situation that was similar.

When Abby was seven years old, we joined a university-model school that met two days each week. We placed her in the kindergarten class, which fit best with her learning level. It was a wonderful year, and she was thriving. All of our kids were thriving, and while it was a lot of work, it seemed right and productive and healthy. The next year started off great as well. Caleb skipped ahead a year, Luke made friends in preschool, and Abby was able to learn alongside other students without modifications in class, just lots of therapy and diligence outside of class.

When Abby began the second semester of first grade, the teacher of the class introduced phonics lessons. Now, you have to understand that I'm not a big fan of the typical phonics methods. Phonics rules might make sense at the beginning, but there are so many exceptions to the rules that it seemed mostly fruitless to learn the rules only to be told to disregard them so often. I preferred to teach reading through mostly sight words. Anyway, it may have been the case that my frustration with trying to teach phonics according to someone else's plans was simply not a good idea. Add in the fact that Abby has Down syndrome, and we had a recipe for disaster. Abby and I began to clash often when it came time to complete the phonics lessons. I was determined to help her keep up with her classmates, but the other students began to read and progress quickly, while Abby seemed to be stuck.

I expressed my frustration to her too many times and I pushed her too hard, until I finally recognized that I needed to take a step away and ask for help. I knew Abby needed grace, patience, and compassion. It was beyond what I thought I could provide at the time. Remember how I mentioned that I struggled with patience? In my intense focus on helping her achieve academic success, I had completely missed seeing her and her true needs. I had lost her trust, and even though I asked for forgiveness, she no longer responded well to my instruction.

Again, I had to be willing to let go in areas where I was weak. I had to admit that I couldn't do everything myself. We decided to try to hire a tutor, at least for a time to allow for some healing and rest. We prayed and asked friends for recommendations, and as had happened before, God already had someone waiting to meet our need. Again and again, God brought people into our lives who answered our cries for help. God blessed us beyond what we could have imagined when he provided the right tutors for Abby.

They were not experts or experienced professionals but women who truly cared about Abby and seemed genuinely excited to learn how to help her and our family. It was beautiful that I was still able to direct their activities and guide Abby's learning, but also step away and let go of the part that was beyond my capabilities at the time.

Protection and Priorities

Letting go is not easy, especially for those of us who like to be in control. (Isn't that all of us?) One of the challenges in parenting is the continual process of letting go. With every milestone and step of progress that our child achieves, we must release a little more of our control. When we pour our lives and so much of our time and attention and effort into caring for our children, and we care so deeply about their well-being, we may have a tendency to become overly protective. Most of us are familiar with the labels that have often been placed on parents who hover too much over their children or who try to smooth the path for their child or many other ways we can be overly protective and cautious with our kids. Helicopter parenting, lawnmower parenting, tiger parenting... I lost track of all the negative labels that have been attached to bad parenting styles. Many of those labels demonstrate the difficulty of letting go.

Having a child with special needs adds another element to this desire to be overly protective. Tyce and I have fought against our natural tendency to overprotect Abby, and we may sometimes go too far in the opposite direction as a result. We know Abby needs more oversight than other young adult women. But we also want her to become as independent as possible. Finding the right balance of how much to let go and how much to continue to guide has been a challenge. Even the most simple and routine things in life may still require some oversight for Abby, such as portion sizes with meals. Abby likes to eat, and one of her physical characteristics is that she cannot easily feel when her belly is full. Because of this, she still needs some assistance in her meal preparation and portion sizes. Thankfully, she recognizes this need and is willing to receive and accept our guidance—most of the time, anyway.

> Finding the right balance of how much to let go and how much to continue to guide has been a challenge.

We desire to guide her with gentleness so she will continue to recognize that our advice is intended to help her and is based out of our love for her. She strives to be diligent in eating correct portion sizes, and she readily reports to us the choices she makes on her own when we are not with her. Because she knows we will help her and that we genuinely care for her health, she often appreciates and even desires our guidance and continuing protection.

Abby needs physical protection in ways that our boys don't. She also needs direction to manage her finances in ways that other adult children don't. These are just a couple of examples of areas where we cannot completely let go. But we have tried to provide Abby with as much freedom and ability to make her own choices as possible. Parents who have a child with special needs must help their child find the appropriate level of independence. It's something very individualized. We cannot simply mimic what friends are doing with their child, because Abby's abilities are specific to her and very unique.

As we have coached Abby to develop more freedom and independence, others have questioned whether she really has the ability to be as independent as we allow her to be. Ironically, friends have also questioned whether we were providing too much guidance and oversight. Each area of life requires finding balance and taking risks. We have had to attempt to determine what risks are acceptable and the benefits of taking those risks. When the benefit outweighs the risk, we move forward.

In order to evaluate the risks and benefits, we must establish appropriate priorities. Now that Abby is an adult, one of our priorities is to help her to eventually live independent of us. We know we won't always be here to care for her, that she will likely outlive us someday, and she desires to be somewhat independent of us as an adult who has the capability to do so. We are in the process of trying to help her establish a community of people to support her and a place where she can live safely with roommates. We hope to find a group of people who care for her deeply enough to invest in protecting her and ensuring that her needs are being met. We'd like to help her avoid being dependent on government welfare programs, but instead rely on a much smaller group of people that we know are trustworthy.

Abby's brothers know that overseeing her care will be a responsibility they carry someday. We have taught them, however, that the responsibility is not theirs alone and can be shared with others. We hope that Abby will always have several lifelong friends, to help her brothers care for her when we are no longer able to.

When Abby was a baby and sick so often, we didn't trust many people to help care for her. It was a challenge to find a trustworthy sitter or even feel confident about leaving her in the church nursery. We didn't have much time away from her for date nights or time alone. But we needed date nights! We knew that date nights were important to maintain for our marriage to continue to survive. When we heard about a respite care program at a nearby church, we decided that we needed to give it a try. We entered the church with great hesitancy, but our fears soon gave way to elation. They had doctors and nurses readily available and a screened volunteer who would be with Abby the whole time to help her explore all the wonderful activities, including play-based therapy! It was amazing!

The church was filled with so many of the therapy tools we had been instructed to use with her, and everywhere we looked kids were having such fun while learning and being loved. They even included siblings so we could have a real evening of rest. We were so blessed by this church and the volunteers who helped our family. It was a lifeline for us as it was often the only night each month when we were able to get away from our kids for a date together.

We found out later that this church had partnered with an organization called Joni & Friends to provide this program for families. We have been impressed with the ongoing work of the Joni & Friends community. For those families seeking respite, or individuals who want to get involved in helping, the Joni & Friends website is a great place to start: *https://www.joniandfriends.org/*

It wasn't really much of a risk, but we were so glad we took that risk to sign up for that respite program in a church where we didn't know anyone. We made the choice to make date nights a priority, and Tyce adjusted his work schedule as much as possible to make those dates happen, and I signed us up as soon as I could for the next date night when it became available. Our marriage was a priority that was worth taking the risk of placing our kids in the hands of strangers that first time we participated. The volunteers at that respite program did not remain strangers but soon became good friends. One volunteer in particular developed an immediate and strong bond with Abby, and she remains a close family friend to this day. We have celebrated many birthdays and holidays together with her and are thankful for both the strengthening of our marriage and also the friendship God provided through that respite program.

Because we have seen God meet our needs in the past, we trust that He will continue to meet our needs in the future. We look to Him to help us determine and establish correct priorities and provide everything Abby needs when we cannot.

 Give thanks to the Lord for He is good; for his stead-fast love endures forever.

— Psalm 136:1

Submitting to Another Plan

As we attempt to establish correct priorities, we recognize that we must consider God's priorities for our lives. My plans and priorities may include pressing full speed ahead in pursuit of some personal goal, such as in my desire for Abby to succeed in learning phonics. But I've since learned that if God is not with me in setting and pursuing those goals, all my efforts will be in vain. I should establish goals only after first seeking direction from God, because any goals that are only mine and not His will not be truly productive. I was taught a strong work ethic, taught to be as efficient as possible, taught to avoid being lazy or wasting time.

Unfortunately, as I was praised for my achievements and often awarded for my accomplishments, I also developed a belief that being busy and "productive" was almost an equivalent to being important. As I graduated from high school with the labels of valedictorian and homecoming queen and head cheerleader and first chair in the band, I mistakenly began to believe that I must be better than others.

Our society has valued productivity and rewarded achievement, and it is helpful to recognize that being productive is a necessary aspect of life. The achievements of past generations are to be admired. Working hard to provide for basic needs is obviously essential. But we have come to a point where we have endless possibilities and ways to be "productive." We have moved far beyond meeting basic needs to striving to fulfill our every desire. As a wealthy society, we have a plethora of options available to us, both in work and play. As our oldest son, Caleb, says, "The world is our oyster, and frankly, it can be really annoying." As a young woman full of potential and energy, I wanted to achieve all the things!!

I remember when our kids were little I read a quote from one of the young women that often would babysit for us. As she graduated from high school, she was asked about her hopes for the future. I read how she hoped to not only have a large family and be a good mom but also travel the world and have a successful career. I could identify with her desires, but I also recognized how unrealistic she was for thinking that she could do all those things.

As a mom to three young kids, I felt the reality of how much time each aspect of life required. But I still possessed those desires to fit in as many of the things as I possibly could! I worked faster and harder and stayed as busy as I could trying to achieve as much as I could. The blessing of being young is that you can sustain that level of activity for quite some time. But eventually, I learned that faster and busier is not always better. We probably all know the story of the tortoise and the hare, which helps us consider this reality.

Tyce recognizes that when he was flying F-16s, he had the belief that he was important because of his achievements. They allowed him to pilot a $35-million-dollar aircraft, after all! He also recognized that he was even more valuable than that aircraft, because the existence of an ejection seat proved it. He had begun to place his identity in his achievement and determine his value based on these kinds of indicators. When he began to consider that Abby is valuable regardless of whether she ever accomplishes anything significant in the view of society or whether she is talented or beautiful or intelligent, he began to realize that he is also valuable even if he is no longer able to pilot an expensive aircraft.

He began to see that his identity and value is not dependent on his ability, talent, achievement, youthfulness, or any other such measure. I began to see a difference in how he portrayed himself to others and how he responded to different stresses in life as a result.

His identity and value is not dependent on his ability, talent, achievement, youthfulness, or any other such measure.

A strong work ethic may include not being lazy, but it doesn't mean we have to be stressed out about always pursuing the next thing. If we are pushing aside relationships and people in our attempts to achieve, what are we really achieving? I am still learning the best methods to manage my time in such a way to avoid being lazy (or allowing my kids to be lazy) but still allow time for relationships and focus on the priority of caring for people. Because Abby often takes more time to complete tasks, I must continually remind myself that faster and busier is not always better. In my attempts to be productive, I can act in ways that are hurtful towards her if I fail to maintain the right attitude and perspective. My attitude and the words I speak towards her can have tremendous impact.

It can be helpful to ask: what does it mean to be productive? Though the hare was fast, did his speed help him accomplish anything worthwhile? In the same way, I can be very busy while accomplishing very little. Sometimes, I recognize that I like to feel busy because it makes me feel important. As the hare was overconfident, we can often become overconfident when we are busy running from one activity to the next, thinking we are being SO productive and therefore must also be important.

> It can be helpful to ask:
> what does it mean
> to be productive?

As a family, we have often visited residents in nearby nursing homes. Our visits to the nursing home often reminded me that being busy and accomplishing tasks is not what life is all about. The residents there engage in activities that are valuable, even though much of the world would consider them unproductive. They demonstrate love to each other. They appreciate beauty and bring joy to one another. They pray for and care for each other and for other family members and friends. Their lives are important.

In that familiar story of the tortoise and the hare, the tortoise remained faithful and steady and consistent. He was not hurried or rushed or unkind as he continued to proceed toward the finish line. We can demonstrate the importance of having these same characteristics and living this way. I recognize this in my role as a mother. One of my current roles in life is to be chauffeur to my kids in all their activities. Because I am naturally a "homebody" and also a "time optimist," it can be a challenge for me to leave the house and get out the door when it's time to go somewhere. I always think I can accomplish one more task before it's time to leave. As a result, I often leave later than I should and then inevitably try to make up time on the way to where we're going. I've learned that this is not a good habit. While I may just want to get where we're going as quickly as possible, I have learned that it is better to relax and actually enjoy the drive, talk along the way, be selfless towards other drivers, and of course, I know we will be safer when I follow the speed limit. I've also learned that most attempts to hurry while driving aren't actually effective in reducing the time it takes to get there!

We can live simply and live well. My natural tendency to hurry, to fill my schedule with as many activities as possible may often be in conflict with what God wants for my life. God often calls me to slow down, to be still and know that He is God. My efforts to accomplish anything on my own are completely fruitless without Him. When I recognize this truth, I can rest and allow God to lift burdens off my shoulders. He carries the weight of our burdens. We don't have to carry them ourselves. Allow Him to take your burdens off your shoulders, and He will carry them for you.

For this is the love of God, that we keep his commandments. And his commandments are not burdensome. For everyone who has been born of God overcomes the world. And this is the victory that has overcome the world - our faith. Who is it that over-comes the world except the one who believes that Jesus is the Son of God?

— 1 John 5:3-5

Be still and know that I am God. I will be exalted among the nations, I will be exalted in the earth.

— Psalm 46:10

It is in vain that you rise up early and go late to rest, eating the bread of anxious toil; for he gives to his beloved sleep.

— Psalm 127:2

Alex and Brett Harris wrote a book together when they were teenagers titled *Do Hard Things*. Since writing that book, these brothers graduated from college and married and have begun their careers. They recently recorded a podcast titled, "*14 Years of Doing Hard Things with Alex and Brett Harris.*"[2] On this podcast (at about minute 13), after discussing some of the difficulties they have encountered, Alex Harris states, "The small hard things are some-times the hardest... Faithfulness in the small things that don't get attention or that may not even be seen by most, if anyone, are truly the hardest things that really go to what it means to be faithful, because it's easy to be excited about doing things that get you acco-lades." Brett says, "Whether there is ever any recognition or any sort of harvest visible that this world recognizes...God is looking for that heart that desires faithfulness to Him... It may not look like some-thing successful in this life, but it absolutely is a sure promise from the Lord." They say their dad always taught: "Faithfulness in one season prepares you to step into the next season with strength."

When I focus on God's priorities, and make His priorities my own, then I am truly productive in ways that matter for eternity. Whether the tasks before us are recognized by others or not, it is our faithfulness and obedience that matters. You may be nursing a child in the darkness of night, feeling tired and alone, but God sees the work you are doing. You may be patiently enduring days of tedious tasks that seem to never end, but God knows the end result and the reward for your labor. You may be at a place in life where it seems there is no hope for the future, but God is accomplishing His perfect plan.

> If I speak in the tongues of men and of angels, but have not love, I am a noisy gong or a clanging cymbal. And if I have prophetic powers, and understand all mysteries and all knowledge, and if I have all faith, so as to remove mountains, but have not love, I am nothing. If I give away all I have, and if I deliver up my body to be burned, but have not love, I gain nothing. Love is patient and kind; love does not envy or boast; it is not arrogant or rude. It does not insist on its own way; it is not irritable or resentful.
>
> — 1 Corinthians 13:1-5

> Trust in the Lord with all your heart, and do not lean on your own understanding. In all your ways acknowledge him, and he will make straight your paths.
>
> — Proverbs 3:5–6

 # For Further Reflection

- What ways have you found to be creative that you enjoy?
- Can you name at least two or three people in your life who are willing to sacrifice their time to help you rest when needed?
- Are there areas of your life where, or are you in the midst of a time when, you need to ask for help?
- How have you seen God meet your needs for rest in the past? Do you trust Him to meet your needs again in the future?
- Do you believe that being more productive indicates that you are also more valuable?
- Do you find yourself feeling stressed about achieving some goal and pushing aside relationships? Do you view your own value and identity as being dependent on what you do or achieve?
- Do you find yourself becoming quickly impatient when you have to wait on others or when others get in your way of accomplishing tasks? In what ways do you react, and how does your reaction affect those around you?
- What expectations do you possess that are unnecessary or completely erroneous? How can you eliminate those expectations?
- Are you carrying burdens that you don't need to carry? How can you release those burdens and give them to God?

Chapter 5

Courageous and Contagious

Standing Out | Being Different

As a family, we have learned that standing out and being different is something we can enjoy and be proud of. We wear the label of "weird" or "abnormal" with honor and pride. I find it ironic how often I read some encouragement to "be yourself" or "be unique," but often in the same setting, we are asked to all conform to some standard. In large groups, we often recognize an underlying understanding that everyone should look or act or think in a certain way. "Groupthink" can be very harmful, and our family enjoys standing up against these prevailing mindsets because we recognize the harm they cause.

We enjoy being different and knowing that we stand out, because it provides a freedom to think for ourselves, to discern what is really true rather than feeling pressure to conform. Actually, I have stated that backwards. It's not that being different gives us freedom. Rather, choosing freedom, choosing to think for ourselves gives us the ability to enjoy being unique. It's when we know that we are pursuing what is true and when we have confidence from knowing that we are living out what is true that we then enjoy the fact that we stand out. We made the choice to have Abby when others would have chosen otherwise.

It's when we know that we are pursuing what is true, and when we have confidence from knowing that we are living out what is true, that we then enjoy the fact that we stand out.

We have made choices to live differently because we knew it was right. Because we know Abby is made in the image of God and we know that her life has value, because we have confidence that we made the right choice, we can enjoy the ways she is different and how our life is different as a result of having her.

> I appeal to you therefore, brothers, by the mercies of God, to present your bodies as a living sacrifice, holy and acceptable to God, which is your spiritual worship. Do not be conformed to this world, but be transformed by the renewal of your mind, that by testing you may discern what is the will of God, what is good and acceptable and perfect.
>
> — Romans 12:1-2

Embrace the FUN Part

Abby loves watching movies. Our sons have watched many of the same movies, and they often quote favorite lines that were particularly funny. Abby has a way of quoting movies at the perfect moment to make a unique point from her unique perspective. Only those who understand the way she thinks, who know the movie reference, or who explore the connection will find the humor. Those who understand can recognize just how hilarious these connections can be! Abby often makes us laugh because she sees things from a different perspective.

Our family has often laughed when particular phrases from Acts 2:2 and John 3:8 are referenced. Acts 2 describes the Holy Spirit as having a "sound like a mighty rushing wind" and in John 3, the movement of the Spirit is described as: "The wind blows where it wishes, and you hear its sound, but you do not know where it comes from or where it goes." Somehow, perhaps from one of the children's versions of the Bible that we read together, the two verses merged into something like "There was a great rushing wind, and no one knew from where it came." Abby suggested that someone may have eaten too many Holy Spirit beans. We weren't sure if she said "being" or "bean," but either way, the memory has stuck!

One thing I love about Abby is that she is so sweet and humble and quiet about her unique gifts and abilities. She doesn't flaunt her differences or promote herself as special, but she recognizes that every person is special in their own way. Because Abby understood that she was created to be a unique individual with a unique purpose, when she was old enough to recognize that she has Down syndrome and was different than most people in this way, she was able to accept that fact without any frustration or confusion.

When I asked her about this recently and asked whether she remembers the moment when she realized that she had Down syndrome and what it means to have Down syndrome, she quoted John 1:13 and said, "For we are born not of blood nor the will of man but the will of God." Abby knows it is God who made her and gave her Down syndrome, and she trusts completely in the fact that He knows what He is doing! She now sometimes calls herself "God's Secret Weapon" as she recognizes the unique opportunities He has given her through having Down syndrome.

When I think about the individuals that I know personally who have unique needs, I smile. I know these individuals as being fun-loving, encouraging people who make others laugh and smile regularly. One young woman who also has Down syndrome is admired by a large community of people because of her outgoing and fun-loving nature and unique perspective of life.

My friend Geri Green recently told me this story about a time that her daughter, Emily, brought a unique kind of joy to her day: "One morning when Emily was in middle school, we had a particularly rough time getting up and ready for the day. We got through bath time, getting dressed, eating breakfast, brushing hair and teeth, but each step made us both a little more grumpy than we'd been before, for no discernible reason. By the time we got in the car for the drive to school, we were barely speaking to each other. (Perhaps you've had a day like this? I'm told we are not the only ones!) A popular movie at that time was Alvin and the Chipmunks, the animated version that featured humans alongside the digitally produced Alvin, Simon, and Theodore. In that movie, the three rodent brothers watch a National Geographic video about meerkats in which they heard the narrator talk about what a struggle survival could be for such tiny creatures living in the wild.

So on that grumpy morning, after we'd been riding quietly in the car for several minutes, Emily suddenly blurted out a line she borrowed from Theodore. She said, 'I am sick of struggling for survival!' I couldn't help myself; I laughed out loud. Then she laughed, too, and just like that, everything was okay. I'll never really know what she actually meant, but I think it must've been something like, 'I'm tired of fussing with one another. Can we just be friends?' If God didn't give Emily the gift of eloquence, he certainly gave her the gift of timing, and this was one instance when I was particularly grateful for it."

I have observed other blessings that go beyond laughter and enjoyment of unique ways of thinking. Another young woman we know has had a tremendous impact on her family and the community around them. In a conversation I had with her mother, here is how her mother described her:

"Ashley's at a toddler level in her development. What she offers are character traits like contentment. She doesn't know to yearn for more or a different life, and she's blessed to not understand that she's disabled. It's hard to care for her day in and day out—almost 24/7—but having her as my responsibility teaches me how to love unconditionally. She teaches me what pure joy is like when she smiles at me. She teaches me that God is in control and to trust Him more. She is the picture of pure innocence. It helps me have an eternal perspective and helps me look forward to a day in heaven when she will be able wrap her arms around me and say with her own mouth what she was thinking all those years. It will be such a joy to have a daughter without limitations one day.

"She has introduced me to a world I never knew existed before she was born, the world of disability and what that does to families. I am able to minister to other young families who have a child with her same gene mutation, CDK19, like no one else is able to. Because I have gone before them, I can sympathize like no other. The other young families that I am in a group with are like my families. We have such a connection because there are only a few that can understand the disappointment that their child will be so profoundly disabled. I am blessed to be able to minister to them. Perhaps they will see Jesus in us. I hope they can.

"I don't know why this happened to us, but God knows. I can only trust that His plan for our lives is bigger than my little ant perspective. God is good, and I see Him in Ashley."

Unique challenges can create unique depth in relationships and emotions. Friendships that develop out of these challenges are deep and meaningful.

We also benefit from observing the generosity of others. Because Down syndrome is outwardly visible, others often take notice of Abby and respond to her. Some people have such a heart of compassion and generosity that they immediately want to reach out to her and bless her. It is not unusual for us to be in a restaurant or out shopping and have someone pay for our meal or buy Abby a toy or stuffed animal. We've started calling it "the Abby effect." It's such a sweet reminder of how many people are kind and caring and generous to strangers. The first few times this happened, I was surprised by it and wanted to tell the person that it was really unnecessary. What I've realized is that those individuals receive joy from giving, and it's not my place to take away the joy they receive from giving to Abby. I now simply enjoy watching as Abby and these generous individuals interact, and I find joy in it as well.

Our family has received many blessings because of Abby having Down syndrome. We've taught our boys to enjoy the benefits that come with the added difficulty. We've been able to attend special events and receive discounts that we would not have been given if Abby didn't have Down syndrome. We learned to accept the generosity and help from other individuals and receive it with gladness and thankfulness.

What About Finances?

Many people recognize that there are additional expenses associated with having unique needs such as Down syndrome. While some of the cost of speech therapy, physical therapy, occupational therapy, sensory integration therapy, oral motor therapy, heart surgery, four sets of ear tubes, medications, etc. have been covered by our medical insurance, we still have co-pays and deductibles and many out-of-pocket expenses.

Abby has not always qualified for government assistance, nor did we seek it out. Even just the co-pays for therapies became a significant financial obligation. We believed it was worth every penny for the progress Abby achieved. Because we believed it was worth it, we made the sacrifice.

We tried to duplicate therapy at home as much as possible to help reduce our medical expenses. When we saw the sensory-integration therapist spend forty-five minutes in a therapy session simply spinning Abby in a rotating swing, we immediately went and found a similar swing that we installed on our back porch. We also purchased a Sit-N-Spin, which she enjoyed for many hours! I also purchased the book The Out-Of-Sync Child,[1] which helped me identify many practical techniques that we were able to implement at home. Some of these techniques were helpful with our boys as well! It was frustrating to realize that therapy was not affordable without insurance or government assistance. While I understand that there is now a great amount of training involved in identifying the needs of each child and choosing the best activities to address those needs, it seems to me that there are many ways that the cost of therapy could be reduced.

The systems of healthcare providers and government welfare programs seem to promote an increase in costs that keeps families and individuals in a perpetual state of dependence. I understand how difficult it can be to break free from that system and find alternative ways to provide the care that a child needs without depending on government. I believe it is imperative for our society to find these alternate ways of providing care that don't depend on government programs.

Many of the exercises and activities that therapists would recommend seemed quite simple. They seemed like pointers that may have been routinely passed down from generation to generation in the past, but in our generation, we have formalized the process and created complete education and healthcare industries that require participation and involve significant costs.

As a stay-at-home mom I did not generate any income to help with expenses. Tyce did feel an increased amount of pressure to maintain a stable job and provide a solid income for our family. This isn't uncommon, of course, and men can respond with either a greater dedication to their family or a hopelessness that can lead to despair and resignation.

When we were in the midst of this season of Abby having such great need for therapy in her formative years, we also experienced a significant cut to Tyce's salary. As a result of the events of September 11, 2001, his income was cut by about a third. Thankfully, we had already been following biblical guidelines for our finances, and we had reserve funds that helped us through this time. We have always been fairly frugal and now made additional choices to avoid spending on unnecessary items.

It was around this time that we moved to a new community in order to be closer to work and family and what we thought were better schools. We were amazed at the amount of money banks were willing to lend us for a new home loan. We knew we didn't really need such a large, nice home, and we chose instead to purchase something smaller that we knew we could afford. This decision and others like it helped to alleviate some of the stress associated with Abby's additional medical bills for therapy and surgery and such.

In spite of the fact that I was not working and generating income, we always felt rich. Because we had utilized biblical principles of finances that we had learned primarily through Crown Financial Ministries,[2] we never felt that we were in need or could not provide what our children needed. In fact, we were able to provide beyond what they needed and cover the costs for horseback riding and sailing and even some really wonderful vacations.

We all make choices as to what is most important to us, and the way we use money is a reflection of that. Our choice was to place higher priority on relationships with our children and providing for their wide variety of needs (including emotional and spiritual) and to ensure that our family and our home provided them with stability and fun and peace. We knew that, just as God had provided answers to our prayers for other things, God would provide for our financial needs as well. We taught our kids the difference between needs and wants. We may have wanted a pool or a new boat or the latest in clothing and fashion, but we didn't need those things. We had to make choices about what we knew was most important.

In following God's principles for our finances, we experienced the blessings of more than just our financial needs being met. Our kids were able to participate in unique activities that helped them develop confidence, and our family was able to create many fun memories, all while knowing that we were not overspending or wasting funds on things that were not helpful or needed. We developed greater trust in God's provision as we experienced blessings from implementing the principles found in His Word.

We have observed other parents who have developed an even greater trust in God for their financial provision. Durenda Wilson and her husband recently shared how their faith and trust in God increased through years of homeschooling eight children on one salary. Durenda tells how her children developed creativity as they learned to utilize what they had available, and she shares an example of how their kids would float down a river in an old plastic 50-gallon barrel. She notes that her kids didn't need an expensive canoe or kayak, but they created wonderful and unique memories from learning to be resourceful.[3]

♥ ♥ ♥

> Blessed is the man who fears the Lord, who greatly delights in His commandments! His offspring will be mighty in the land; the generation of the upright will be blessed. Wealth and riches are in his house.

— Psalm 112:1b-3a

> The reward for humility and fear of the Lord is riches and honor and life.

— Proverbs 22:4

> The one who trusts in the Lord will be enriched.

— Proverbs 28:25

> But if we have food and clothing, with these we will be content.

— 1 Timothy 6:8

> Keep your life free from love of money, and be content with what you have, for He has said, "I will never leave you nor forsake you." So we can confidently say, "The Lord is my helper. I will not fear."

— Hebrews 13:5-6

Imagine Not Worrying About Image

Tyce has told me about how concerned he was as a young man with being "cool." When he first became a pilot, he had intentions of living a life that others would envy. He had intended to purchase an expensive watch for himself and live in a beautiful home and always look good. His mindset has changed so much now that I find it difficult to believe he once thought this way. Tyce no longer worries about being "cool." He is no longer very concerned with outward appearances or what others think of him. In fact, he now enjoys being "uncool" and challenging that prevailing attitude that being cool is something we should value.

When our kids were little and we often went to parks, they would ask us to play with them. Most other parents would stand off to the side, perhaps talking with other adults or looking at something on their iPhone, but Tyce was always ready to join in the fun with the kids. I often played with them as well, but Tyce realized that there is part of him that still enjoys being a kid, so he always joined in. He didn't worry about whether he looked silly to the other adults that were there.

Tyce values our kids, and his willingness to play is a reflection of how much he cares for them. He would rather make them happy than look "cool." He would rather be seen as a fool himself than ignore the needs and desires of his kids. He has chosen what he knows is right and his choice gives him the freedom to enjoy playing with our kids just about anywhere. He has had so much fun, and it keeps him in great shape too! If we worry so much about presenting some image that others will accept, we might miss out on many moments of joy. Instead, we can choose to focus on what we know is right and good and live in that joyful confidence.

I remember as a child often wearing hand-me-downs from my sister or other friends. This seemed to be quite common, and class photos from that time indicate to me that back then there was overall less emphasis in our society on outward appearance. Hand-me-downs were common as opposed to the new, trendy clothing that is so prevalent among kids today. As we now experience increasing inflation and as many explore minimalist trends, perhaps we as a society will return to simpler practices where hand-me-downs are once again an accepted norm and outward image is not such a focus. As we consider the future for Abby, we recognize that she may not always have nice, new clothes or furniture or decorations in her home. Her financial situation may not allow her to buy beautiful new things, but she can learn to be content with a simpler life. In fact, she is already content with a simpler life, and I can learn from her example in this. When she earns a wage or receives a financial gift, her typical response is to think of some way that she can use it to give to others. If you give her a gift card to a restaurant, her first thought will be about who she can take with her.

Abby knows her identity as a child of God. She knows her identity as an accepted and deeply loved member of our family. I hope she will also always know that she is loved and accepted by those in her church. It is my desire that she will find where she fits in our church and community without feeling any pressure to conform to a certain image or exhibit a certain level of beauty. I hope she will be loved for her personality, for the unique way she thinks, for the joy she exhibits, for the encouragement she brings, for the way she prays and has genuine concern for others, for the contentment she portrays, and simply because she is made in the image of God.

When we consider what we are known for in our communities, do we focus on our outward appearance or achievements? When we describe our kids to others, do we describe them according to what they do and what activities they are engaging in, or do we describe them by the choices they make and the character they exhibit? We should see ourselves and each person as an individual who has value that is not based on what we might accomplish, not on how we look or some talent or ability we possess, but instead see that we are valuable because of who we are. We are each a creation of a loving God who does not make mistakes, and as such, we are inherently valuable. Instead of focusing on external measurements for determining the value of an individual, I hope we will place emphasis on the intrinsic value of each person and their personality, character, and eternal nature as a unique being who is created in the image of God.

We are each a creation of a loving God who does not make mistakes, and as such, we are inherently valuable.

 Even a child makes himself known by his acts, by whether his conduct is pure and upright.

— Proverbs 20:11

Scaling Schoolwork

We don't always understand the way Abby's mind functions. I'm convinced that we could research the brains of those who have Down syndrome and discover some amazing new pathways and connections that would benefit us all. We have always believed that God created Abby with wonderful gifts and abilities. Finding those gifts and abilities is sometimes like going on a search for hidden treasure.

When Abby was just beginning to be able to express her desires with words, we began to really discover her unique way of thinking. Tyce was helping to heat her food during mealtime one day and

Abby kept telling him, "Daddy, make it warm." So Tyce kept heating the food, only to have her again say that she wanted it warm. She said, "No, daddy, I want it WARM!" Finally, Tyce realized that what she meant is that the food was too hot, and she wanted it warm, not hot. It was a different way of communicating that he wasn't used to, but the way she stated her request was completely accurate and actually more accurate than the way we were accustomed to communicating.

We've learned that Abby takes our words more literally. Even now, when we attempt to be sarcastic, she often thinks we are being serious. We have to be careful to recognize when we might need to explain that we are merely joking.

Throughout Abby's education, we have recognized the need to reduce new concepts into smaller segments. Our boys often skipped steps, but with Abby, we often added extra steps and included extra practice. When Luke skipped over the extra math problems or sections of curriculum that were intended for review, we used those for additional practice for Abby.

It was wonderful when other people helped us or learned how to help us make accommodations for Abby. The kids had a wonderful piano teacher, Mrs. Wren, who took the time to create unique, handwritten music to meet Abby's need for simplified lessons. Mrs. Wren also recognized that Abby was diligent in practicing every day. She praised Abby and used Abby's diligence as an example for other students to emulate. It was such a joy to receive Mrs. Wren's kindness and generosity towards Abby and our family.

Abby's last year of formal education was filled with exciting challenges. We participated in a program called Classical Conversations,[4] and Abby was very diligent in working to accomplish every assignment listed in the curriculum. She wanted to check off every item on the list and complete every task as it was assigned. I soon learned to modify the assignment list before giving it to her. Even typical students didn't complete every assignment, but Abby tried with all her might to finish everything. Even after I modified the assignment list and told her that she didn't have to complete everything, she still spent all day long working on those assignments. I was eventually able to convince her of ways that she could modify the assignments in order to complete them in a more reasonable amount of time. For example, she traced the maps rather than attempting to draw them freehand.

Abby had high standards for herself, and we encouraged her to work to the best of her ability. As I directed the classroom of students, she heard me instruct the students to complete the assignments to the best of their ability, and she took that instruction seriously. She would often become frustrated when she couldn't complete an assignment. We wanted her to learn to follow through and complete what she was told to do, but we also had to help her understand that there is grace and accept that adjustments that were sometimes necessary. We wanted her to learn that she could adjust the goal, as long as it was adjusted according to her natural ability rather than adjusted for lack of effort.

Abby worked very hard and was successful in many ways as a result of her hard work. She even won first place in the science fair! At the end of the year, when she no longer had assignments to complete, she continued to apply this same level of diligence to the tasks she really enjoyed.

She now studies the Bible intensely and memorizes lengthy Scripture passages. She has memorized the whole book of Ruth and recited it for large groups. She learned to persevere through trials and developed character which portrays hope to others.

Not only that, but we rejoice in our sufferings, knowing that suffering produces endurance, and endurance produces character, and character produces hope, and hope does not put us to shame, because

> God's love has been poured out into our hearts
> through the Holy Spirit who has been given to us.
>
> — Romans 5:3-5

Independence and Dependence

When Abby turned sixteen, we started to teach her to drive. We took her to my parents' farm where they had four-wheelers and a golf cart and plenty of room to navigate without too many obstacles. We taught Abby the basics of driving and allowed her to explore her abilities. It wasn't long before she decided for herself that driving was beyond her ability and that she did not feel safe driving. We helped her put words to her thoughts and to recognize that the mental processes needed for driving had to be done more rapidly than what her brain was able to process. She accepted her limitations, and as far as we know, she never felt a need to grieve over that recognition that she may never drive. It was simply how God created her and a reality of her life that she accepted.

We have been so thankful that Abby has accepted the limitations that God has placed on her. She has allowed us to help her with many decisions, as she recognizes her own limitations. She depends on us willingly when she knows she needs our help, and she trusts us to make decisions that are based out of our love for her and our desire to do what is best for her.

One of the reasons Abby may not feel a need to grieve over her limitations is because we have never placed a huge emphasis on those milestones that others consider significant. We have simply taken one step at a time towards progress and towards achieving the next goal, but we have avoided comparing Abby's achievements to others. Because we educate at home, we were able to avoid any overemphasis on certain milestones or traditions or expectations.

Abby has a wonderful understanding of how we all depend on each other. She knows others depend on her prayers and benefit from her encouragement. She sees how each member of our family depends on each other. While Tyce and I grew up thinking that complete independence was the goal, we've taught our kids that depending on God is the better goal.

> We've taught our kids
> that depending on God
> is the better goal.

When Abby was a newborn and still in the hospital, Tyce spent many hours driving back and forth to the hospital. On one of these drives, he was feeling the weight of the burden of having to provide for our family and all of Abby's needs. As he was praying about this, he suddenly remembered that he was not alone. He remembered that he had a wife who was happy to have Abby and care for her and meet her needs. He realized that he could depend on me. And later, he realized that he could also depend on others as well. He did not have to be completely independent and feel the burden of providing everything himself.

 For I, the Lord your God, hold your right hand; it is I who say to you, "Fear not, I am the one who helps you."

— Isaiah 41:13

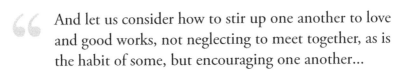

> And let us consider how to stir up one another to love
> and good works, not neglecting to meet together, as is
> the habit of some, but encouraging one another...

— Hebrews 10:24-25

> As each has received a gift, use it to serve one another,
> as good stewards of God's varied grace.

— 1 Peter 4:10

Love Like Family

We hope Abby can avoid becoming dependent on government
programs. While we recognize some positive aspects of these
programs, we hope that God will provide a community of people
who value Abby like we do, who see the blessings of having her in
their lives as we do, who want her in their lives and enjoy what she
adds to their lives and their community in the same way that we do.
Government programs are not usually administered in such a way
to create long-term, committed relationships with depth of care
that results from unconditional love. I am thankful that so many in
our nation have voted to help provide for the needy through
government programs, and I recognize that some programs are
essential, but we must realize that government cannot ever replace
the family or the church, nor should it attempt to do so.

We are in process of searching for people who love Abby and
desire to invest in and commit to helping with her long-term care. I
can't write the end of this story and wrap it up with a nice conclu-
sion of how God has provided. We are still in the midst of praying
and asking the questions: Will we find people who care for Abby
without having to be paid to do it? Will Abby find a community of
friends who love her enough to sacrifice for her? Will we find others
who value her, love her, enjoy her and want her in their lives like we

do? Because I have seen God answer our prayers in the past, because I know He cares for her more than I do, I have confidence that He will provide for her in His way and His time. I don't need to be anxious or force a result, but I can rest and have peace as I trust God to provide.

There is a special bond parents have with their children. I know that others do not have a history with Abby like we do. A family is a unique institution that cannot be easily duplicated. Am I unrealistic to expect that the same bonds we share as family can be duplicated by friends and others? Is this even a good thing to desire?

In 1880, Dutch prime minister Abraham Kuyper spoke about Sphere Sovereignty,[5] and much has been discussed and debated on this topic since then. Kuyper asks the question: "Is that all-embracing Sovereignty of God delegated undivided to one single man; or does an earthly Sovereign possess the power to compel obedience only in a limited circle; a circle bordered by other circles in which another is Sovereign?" He states, "There is also a domain of the personal, of the domestic, of the scientific, of the social, and of the ecclesiastical life; each of which obeys its own law of life, and each subject to its own head." This could be discussed in much greater depth, but for our purpose here, I would designate these three spheres of authority that we could all recognize: family provides one sphere of authority, church provides another, and government provides another.

These are distinct spheres of sovereignty, each with its own set of rules and its own leaders. The question here is this: do theses spheres of sovereignty ever overlap? When, if ever, does the church or the government step into the position of acting on behalf of the family?

In what instances and circumstances does (or should) the state have authority in family matters? Likewise, when does the church act in the place of the family? When do these circles overlap and who then is the sovereign and what rules apply? Perhaps we can look to the Bible for a glimpse into the answer.

When we choose to believe in Jesus Christ as our Lord and Savior, we become members of a new family. God adopts us as His children. I believe the Bible uses this terminology for a reason. There are times when the church functions as our family. God is described in Psalm 68 as being "father to the fatherless and protector of widows." The church is the body through which He acts in this way.

God has blessed me with a wonderful biological family. My parents brought me up with love and kindness and taught me truth. My husband and my children fill my days with joy and love. There is a unique bond that we share that provides peace and security through unconditional acceptance and unending forgiveness. We feel comfortable enough to share personal struggles, to be physically close, and we are also bound by a mostly unspoken commitment to drop everything and help when one of us has a need. I recognize that some people don't have this same blessing in their biological family. This is why adoption is such a beautiful concept.

Through adoption, those who are alone can have these same bonds of love, joy, commitment, security. Adoption in the legal sense secures a commitment to a child's physical needs and hopefully also addresses and attempts to fulfill the child's emotional needs as well, for a lifetime.

When we are adopted into God's family, we have access to the endless riches of the King of Kings, the boundless love of the God who knows everything about us, the continual presence and comfort of the God who is everywhere, the impenetrable security and provision of the God who created and owns everything, and the eternal joy of the God who delights in us and desires to give us what He knows will fulfill our deepest desires.

God is Sovereign over all. He has power and authority over everything, yet He does delegate authority to earthly leaders. Romans 13 tells us how He establishes governments with authority to administer punishment to the evildoer. Ephesians 5 tells us that the husband is established as the head of the family. 1 Timothy 3 designates elders as leaders in the church. One of the ways God demonstrates His love towards us is through other members of His family. We become brothers and sisters in Christ, and often these bonds in our Christian family become even stronger than the bonds we have with our biological family. I see Abby developing these kinds of bonds with others in our church, and I have faith that God will provide for her through His family when needed. Do I expect the church to replace our family in Abby's life? Of course not.

> One of the ways God demonstrates His love towards us is through other members of His family.

I don't expect the church to provide all her needs and care for her as someone fully dependent for her sustenance. But if needs arise someday that our family cannot meet, I hope there will be a community of people from our church to step in and take on that role.

> Do not forsake your friend and your father's friend, and do not go to your brother's house in the day of calamity. Better is a neighbor who is near than a brother who is far away.
>
> — Proverbs 27:10

Rest, Delight, and Beauty

Our nature is to seek our own happiness, to enjoy beauty, to find rest. The pursuit of happiness, along with life and liberty, is written into the founding documents of our nation as one of our most basic rights. God tells us clearly the secret to happiness. Psalm 37:4 gives us a command with a promise: "Delight yourself in the LORD, and He will give you the desires of your heart."

Abby delights in God, and her enjoyment of God causes others to delight in Him as well. Her simple faith reminds me that I don't have to complicate my faith; I don't have to have all the answers. God doesn't need efforts or sacrifices that come from our own strength (1 Samuel 15:22). Instead, He desires that we submit and obey so He can entrust us with more and bless us more. In Matthew 25:14–30, we read that when we are faithful in the small things, we will be given more.

Many passages such as Romans 5, James 1, and 2 Corinthians 4 help us understand that when we persevere through suffering, we receive many blessings and benefits. As I look back over all our experiences, I recognize that God has changed my heart in many ways. What once was important to me now seems shallow and meaningless. Things that I once thought would bring me happiness and joy I now realize only provide some temporary relief from the drudgery of life. But what God has brought into my life through my daughter having Down syndrome is a much greater joy than I could have once imagined.

When I first married Tyce, I expected to travel the world with him. I had grand plans for all the places we would go and things we would see. I mistakenly thought that through travel and adventure, I would find greater happiness. Whether we pursue material wealth, possessions, leisure, adventure, or even strive to attain some measure of success in societal progress or human advancement, none of these will truly satisfy our deepest desires.

I see now that I don't have to concern myself with image,

comfort, productivity, or achievements. I don't have to stress over these, but only do the work God calls me to do and be diligent and obedient. I see that God's plan and the principles described in the Bible really work. When we follow His commands, life is filled with joy and meaning and depth. It is only through Him that our deepest desires can be fulfilled.

The things I have gained from having Abby and from allowing God to change my heart are eternal and bring lasting benefits. I also recognize that any pain or suffering we have experienced has been temporary and light, especially in view of eternity. As 2 Corinthians 4:16–18 says, "So we do not lose heart. Though our outer self is wasting away, our inner self is being renewed day by day. For this light momentary affliction is preparing for us an eternal weight of glory beyond all comparison as we look not to the things that are seen but to the things that are unseen. For the things that are seen are transient, but the things that are unseen are eternal." Through the trials of life, we are gaining eternal benefits and eternal glory that far outweighs any difficulty we might experience here on earth.

> Count it all joy, my brothers, when you meet trials of various kinds, for you know that the testing of your faith produces steadfastness. And let steadfastness have its full effect so that you may be perfect and complete, lacking in nothing.
>
> — James 1:2-4

Blessed is the man who remains steadfast under trial, for when he has stood the test he will receive the crown of life, which God has promised to those who love him.

— James 1:12

Every person on earth has been created to bring glory to God and therefore exhibits beauty. Sometimes, we may not easily recognize this, and we may have to step outside our typical patterns of thought to discover the ways a person brings glory to God or exhibits beauty. We can search for true beauty and find greater depth in our understanding of God as a result. True beauty is not just the surface level beauty of outward appearance but an inner beauty that is eternal.

We're all children in God's eyes, and the Bible calls us to see others the way God sees them. When I view myself and others as children of God, I find that my attitude changes and I eliminate any false pretenses. Children tend to be very straightforward, and most of us enjoy children because of their simplicity of thought and care-free, genuine mindset. Children most often care more about how someone treats them than what someone looks like. They tend to be very trusting and assume the best of others, regardless of how they look on the outside.

There is nothing necessarily wrong with striving to be beautiful both inside and outside, to enjoy making a home look nice, to choose hairstyles and clothing that look pleasant, as long as this is not our primary focus or interferes with higher priorities or causes us to present a façade that is not genuine character. Some individuals are gifted in aspects of life that focus on beauty, and we can recognize that God calls some to focus on this more than others. Artists can help us focus our thoughts on things that are lovely and even convey truth through their craft. In much the same way, the unique needs of some can remind us that the beauty that lasts is beauty that is within. Individuals with unique needs can help us focus on a deeper beauty that goes beyond outward appearances. They exhibit inner beauty that displays truth, and they convey to us all certain truths about God.

We see beauty in how God works out His story in us. If you've learned anything from reading our story, I expect you have learned that we have made mistakes and even made wrong choices sometimes, but God always provides for our needs. No matter what our failures have been, God continues to sustain us and redeem even our poor choices to accomplish His good purposes.

> We see beauty in how God works out His story in us.

Each of us has a unique story. We can allow God to work out His plan in our lives or try to accomplish our own goals. Eventually, we all find out: YOUR story is God's story in you. When we recognize the truth of who God created us to be, how much He loves us, and the plan He has for our lives, we exhibit His beauty more clearly to others. In the same way that those children who were adopted were beautiful because they are loved, you are beautiful because you are loved. God loves you and God loves your child. The more I study who God is and how He has revealed Himself in His Word, the more I discover and recognize His great love!

We can work to eliminate the many things in life that burden us and often cause us to fail to choose correctly or establish right priorities. Throw off the burdens of portraying an outward image or visible achievements, and instead focus on what great love God has lavished on us. When we focus on God's love for us, we will display inner beauty, and when we focus on sharing His love, we will make a much stronger impression on others. The love of God in us will portray a much greater beauty and much stronger love than anything we can produce from our own efforts. God loved us so much that He gave us His only Son to die on the cross so that we might be saved and have eternal life and have abundant life that is full of beauty and love now!

> Therefore, since we are surrounded by so great a cloud of witnesses, let us also lay aside every weight, and sin which clings so closely, and let us run with endurance the race that is set before us, looking to Jesus, the founder and perfecter of our faith, who for the joy that was set before him endured the cross, despising the shame, and is seated at the right hand of the throne of God.
>
> Consider him who endured from sinners such hostility against himself, so that you may not grow weary or fainthearted.
>
> — Hebrews 12:1-3

Purpose Fulfilled

We realize that Abby is currently already fulfilling the purpose God has for her life. Each day, wherever we are, God uses us to accomplish His purposes. I trust that God has a plan for each day, and I don't have to orchestrate every detail or be stressed in my efforts to ensure that any goals I may set will be achieved. Fulfilling my purpose in life is not a particular achievement that comes only after I have reached a certain destination or accomplished a particular task. Children fulfill God's purpose in their lives each day. Elderly people continue to have purpose even after they retire or stop pursuing "productive" types of work. I don't need to worry about Abby "finding" her purpose. As that passage in Matthew 6 states, each day has enough trouble of its own. I don't need to worry about tomorrow but focus on today and only what is needed for today. We can trust God to help us achieve His goals and provide all that we need today. When we know that we are living out our purpose here and now, we don't have to strive for or feel pressured to be something we're not, to do things we don't have the skills to do, to work with strength we don't have. We can rest when we are weary and simply do the best we can at the moment.

Tyce was often tired when he came home from a long and difficult day. When our kids were little, they didn't understand this and still wanted his time and attention. Sometimes being a good dad, for him, was simply lying on the floor and letting the kids jump all over him. When he was obedient to what God was calling him to do, even if it was something as simple as lying on the floor, he fulfilled his purpose in the role in which God had placed him.

Sometimes our purpose in life is simply surviving through the trials and pains of this world. Long-suffering is a fruit produced by the Holy Spirit within us. The way we respond to suffering and trials can in itself accomplish God's purpose. Tyce has often shared with our kids about the individuals he views as heroes. He recognizes that we all need heroes who are real, not celebrities or fictional characters that are completely out of touch with our own reality. We have enjoyed reading many biographies of people that we consider heroes, including those recorded by Janet and Geoff Benge in their "Heroes" series of biographies, published by YWAM. The story of Gladys Aylward[6] was one of the first of these books that we read together, in our first year of homeschooling. Gladys is an example of someone who chose a life of service and sacrifice; she experienced great physical suffering as she cared for more than a hundred orphans and delivered them to safety.

As the kids and I read about Gladys Aylward and others who persevered through suffering, we noticed another benefit of suffering is that it helps us learn to obey. As we read about how these individuals suffered and chose to obey God in spite of great personal sacrifice, we were all encouraged and inspired to be obedient ourselves, even when it meant we must sacrifice. We learned that when we choose to obey in the midst of suffering, God is glorified. Several years ago, when I was in the midst of a particularly difficult time, I was amazed to learn that even Jesus learned obedience through suffering, as described in Hebrews 5:8. After a significant injury due to an automobile accident, I struggled with accepting my new physical reality of chronic pain. As I realized that I would experience ongoing physical suffering myself, I was strengthened by knowing that no matter what pain I might experience, Jesus could relate to and understand my struggle. He suffered beyond anything I will ever experience, and even He learned obedience. Therefore, I can have confidence and rejoice in learning from whatever hardships come along in my life.

> I was strengthened by knowing that no matter what pain I might experience, Jesus could relate to and understand my struggle.

God gives our lives purpose simply by creating us in His image. Abby loves to read her Bible late into the night, and we often tell her not to stay up too late studying. But perhaps her time alone in her room with God, reading His Word and worshiping Him, is just as precious and valuable to God as anything else she might ever do. She may never speak to another crowd of people or record another podcast, but if she simply praises Him and worships Him in the quiet of her own room, she has purpose.

Some good friends of ours, friends we have known and loved for many years, had a baby boy who lived only a few hours here on earth. He was born with Trisomy-18. Though he lived only for a very short time, Isaac made a tremendous impact on many lives. It was obvious that his parents loved him as much as they did their other five children. When we recognize that God delights in watching us fulfill His plan in our lives, whether that is done in a few hours or in a hundred years, we can enjoy each moment and find purpose in each and every event and choice. Every life is valuable and has purpose. Whether we suffer with ongoing pain and difficulty, or we ever accomplish a particular level of education or achievement, or live for only a few hours, our lives have beauty and bring glory to God.

When Abby was little and just beginning to understand some of the most basic aspects of God's character, she asked a lot of questions. One night, as Tyce was administering another breathing treatment, Abby questioned him about where God is. Tyce explained how God is everywhere, that Jesus is with us all the time, and that we can talk to Him anytime we want to. Abby sat straight up in bed and said, "Jesus! Jesus!" Tyce initially started to tell her that Jesus wasn't actually there to have a conversation, but he quickly caught himself and realized that Abby was right. Jesus was right there. He is right here with us always.

Abby's simple childlike faith and acceptance of what her dad told her was lived out with an immediate and trusting response that brought Tyce to tears. As he recognized the reality of what he had just taught Abby, the truth came alive to him and he realized that Jesus was right there with them. Abby continues to exhibit this same childlike faith. She talks with God continually, still trusting in the truth that Tyce taught her years ago. God is with her always, and He hears every word she says. Oh, what joy if we could all have that same acceptance of truth and childlike faith!

❤ 💜 ❤

" And calling to him a child, he put him in the midst of them and said, "Truly, I say to you, unless you turn and become like children, you will never enter the kingdom of heaven. Whoever humbles himself like this child is the greatest in the kingdom of heaven."

— Matthew 18:2-4

 # For Further Reflection

- What do you think of when you see the advice "just be yourself"?
- Do you recognize any ways that you have conformed to "groupthink"? In what ways can "groupthink" be harmful?
- Do you feel freedom to do what you know is right and, as a result, feel freedom to enjoy being different?
- How have you experienced the fun side of people who have different ways of thinking?
- Have you experienced a deeper joy or connection with others as a result of someone having unique needs?
- How have you been able to express personal generosity to someone who had unique needs?
- When you consider government welfare programs, can you identify how they are inefficient, create dependency, and increase our overall costs for medical care?
- Do you agree that it is important for our society to reduce our dependence on government and make government welfare more efficient in order to reduce the costs of medical care?
- Do you follow biblical principles for your finances? Can you name some of the benefits of following biblical principles for finances?
- Do you trust God to provide for your financial needs?
- If you have children or grandchildren, how do you teach them the difference between wants and needs?

- Is it important to be "cool" or to impress others with your outward appearance? How much emphasis do you place on your outward appearance and image?
- Do you place unnecessary expectations on your kids by working towards certain milestones or making too many comparisons to others?
- Do you struggle with feeling like burdens are yours alone?
- Can you identify some of the benefits of being in God's family? Have you been adopted as a child of God?
- In what ways have you seen the church function as a family?
- Do you have bonds with brothers and sisters in Christ that are stronger than your biological family?
- Do you delight in the Lord?
- Do you recognize beauty in others, and know the difference between inner and outer beauty?
- Do you know that God loves your child? Do you know that God loves you?
- When you discover a new truth about God, do you accept it with child-like faith? If not, what hinders you from accepting it? Can you throw off those things that hinder you and become like a child, trusting that God's Word is true?
- Do you believe that God's Word contains principles that really work?
- Have you seen the reality of 2 Peter 1:3 that "His divine power has granted to us all things that pertain to life and godliness, through the knowledge of him who called us to his own glory and excellence"?

Chapter 6

The End of the Matter, When All Has Been Heard: A More Accurate View of Suffering

In John chapter 9, we read about a man born blind. The most impactful statement in the passage is this: "It was not because he or his parents sinned, but in order that God might be glorified." There it is, in black and white. God caused this man to be blind so that He might be glorified.

Some people may see this as a reason to turn away from God. Isn't it selfish for God to inflict suffering on this man, a life of blindness, for the purpose of glorifying Himself? Is it cruel for God to put suffering on us so that He can be praised? Did this man curse God when he learned that God was the one responsible for his blindness? He is not angry when he learns that it was God who has blinded him. Perhaps the man already knew this truth. Instead of being angry with God, he responds with joy. He is not bitter about the life of suffering with blindness that he had experienced up until that moment of healing. Instead, he is grateful for healing. He uses his experience to give others the opportunity to choose to believe in God and become followers.

This world is full of suffering. This book includes examples of how our family experienced times of suffering, but at the end of each one, there is a reason to be thankful. As we look back over each experience that God has brought us through, we respond with praise and joy. In many cases, we can now see how God uses our suffering so that He might be glorified. And we're not angry that He inflicted suffering on us in order that He might be glorified. Instead, we are thankful and joyful that we got to be part of the process.

When suffering ends, when evil is stopped, when pain is relieved, when sorrow turns to joy, the joy is magnified. If we knew only joy, without the pain and suffering, it would be empty. Every good story includes some conflict. God, in His wisdom, knew this and planned it this way. We can be mad at Him for creating this world with pain and suffering, and our anger will serve absolutely no purpose whatsoever. Our anger and rejection of God will only cause our pain and suffering to increase. But if we accept the fact that God is God, and we acknowledge that He has the prerogative to create this world however He wants and to use whatever means He wants and glorify Himself as much as He wants—because He is God, after all—then our suffering will not be in vain. It will not be empty and meaningless. It will result in a joy that is beyond anything we can imagine.

When we seek to help Abby "find purpose," it goes beyond figuring out her strengths and weaknesses and helping her learn how to use the gifts God has given her. We don't really even have to "find" our purpose, it is inherent within who we are. The person who suffers even the greatest pain, who cannot utter a word or move a muscle through their own strength, still glorifies God. By simply being alive, each person brings glory to God. Our weakness, our pain, our sin all points us to God's strength, His righteousness, His holiness. You are a creation of God, made in His image, "doomed" to live in a world filled with suffering and pain that is the result of sin, and you have the option to choose or reject the God who made you and put you here. Reject Him and you will suffer more and suffer immensely. Choose to believe Him and follow Him and you will experience the joy He intended and planned for you from the beginning. He has had a good plan, an eternal reward, planned for you from before you ever began to suffer a moment of pain. He knew that every pain you would suffer has a greater reward, a greater purpose, a greater joy attached to it. This is how He designed and orchestrated it to be. It is not selfish of Him to bring us a greater joy than we would know without pain and suffering. It is not cruel for Him to drag us through a brief life of suffering so that we can experience an eternity of such immense joy that we almost forget the suffering ever existed, but when we do remember it, we give thanks for it and rejoice all the more! No, God is not selfish or cruel. His plan for us is good. He knows the end and the immense joy that results.

The verses upon which we established our family are found in Ephesians 3:14–21:

> For this reason I bow my knees before the Father, from whom every family in heaven and on earth is named, that according to the riches of His glory, he may grant to be strengthened with power through his Spirit in your inner being, so that Christ may dwell in your hearts through faith - that you, being rooted and grounded in love, may have strength to comprehend with all the saints what is the breadth and length and height and depth, and to know the love of Christ that surpasses knowledge, that you may be filled with all the fullness of God. Now to him who is able to do far more abundantly than all we ask or think, according to the power at work within us, to him be glory in the church and in Christ Jesus throughout all generations, for ever and ever! Amen.

What more is there to say? God's love for us is so wide, so long, so high, so deep...it surpasses knowledge. As another version states it, He can do immeasurably more than all we might ask or imagine. He has a greater reward waiting for us that will make every moment of pain and suffering a distant memory that only increases our joy and thankfulness.

Know this is true, believe His Word, choose Him and live! Enjoy the fact that your suffering WILL produce perseverance in you, that your perseverance WILL produce character in you, and that your character WILL produce hope. And know that hope will not disappoint. Have faith that God has a reward waiting for you in heaven that is greater than any pain or suffering you might experience here on earth!

I recently participated in a speech and debate competition as a judge. One speech in particular stands out in my memory. Two young women acted out the story told in the book, *The Hiding Place*.[1] As they portrayed the lives of Corrie and Betsie ten Boom and attempted to communicate the immense suffering experienced during their time in a concentration camp in Nazi Germany, my eyes filled with tears. I watched as they told the story of how Betsie instructed Corrie to give thanks for everything, even the fleas. Corrie could not imagine any reason to give thanks for fleas, but God revealed to them the greater purpose He had in sending the fleas into their barracks. Betsie exhibited joy through every bit of suffering because she trusted that God had a good purpose for it all.

The speech ended with these verses in Romans 8:38–39: "For I am sure that neither death nor life, nor angels nor rulers, nor things present nor things to come, nor powers, nor height nor depth, nor anything else in all creation, will be able to separate us from the love of God in Christ Jesus our Lord."

God's love for us is greater than any pain or suffering that we experience in this world! The beginning of that chapter of Romans 8 tells us that there is no condemnation for those who are in Christ, that we are set free from the law of sin and death! Verse six tells us that a mind controlled by the Spirit is life and peace! Verse eleven tells us that, if Christ is in us, our spirit is alive because of righteousness! If we put to death the misdeeds of the body, as verse seventeen says, we will live and be sons of God, "heirs of God and fellow heirs with Christ, provided we suffer with him in order that we may also be glorified with him."

Paul writes in verse 18: "For I consider that the sufferings of this present time are not worth comparing with the glory that is to be revealed to us." And in verse 24, he writes, "Now hope that is seen is not hope. For who hopes for what he sees? But if we hope for what we do not see, we wait for it with patience." And finally, in verse 37, we are told, "In all these things

we are more than conquerors through him who loved us." In Christ, through His great love for us, we can rise above the pain and suffering of this world and have hope!

Epilogue

This is my prayer for you, that you will have hope and know the joy that Betsie Ten Boom displayed in the midst of great suffering. I pray that you will allow the suffering of this world to help you develop perseverance and character and hope. I pray you will choose to believe that God has a good plan for your future that will make every moment of suffering someday be a distant memory that brings joy and thankfulness.

If you want to know more about how to have this hope, start with this: read the Bible. The book of John is a good place to begin. It tells the history of how Jesus came from heaven to earth to demonstrate God's great love to us. You can begin to understand who Jesus is as you read about His life here on earth.

John 3:16 says that God so loved the world that he gave his one and only Son so that whoever believes on him will not perish but will have eternal life.

Romans 3:23 tells us that all of us have sinned and fall short of the glory of God. Without Christ and as a result of our sin, we experience death.

Romans 6:23 states that the wages of sin (what we earn through our sin) is death. But the free gift of God is eternal life in Christ Jesus our Lord.

Jesus says in John 14:6, "I am the way and the truth and the life. No one comes to the Father except through me."

1 John 1:9 tells us that if we confess our sins, God is faithful and just and will forgive us of our sins and cleanse us from all unrighteousness.

You can talk directly to God. Through Christ, we have access to God, the Father. Simply tell God that you believe in Jesus, His Son, as He is described in the Bible, being without sin and born of a virgin. Tell God that you believe that Jesus came from heaven to earth to demonstrate God's love to us, and that you believe Jesus died on the cross to take the punishment for your sins. Admit that you are a sinner, ask God to forgive your sins, and tell him that you receive the free gift of salvation that He is offering to you. Invite God to be your Lord and give Him control of your life. Acknowledge that God's plan for your life is better than any plan you might have for yourself and choose to follow His path for your life.

You won't regret it!! Find a church where you can grow and learn and be encouraged and strengthened in your faith. Live in the love and joy and hope that comes from being cleansed of sin and trusting God!

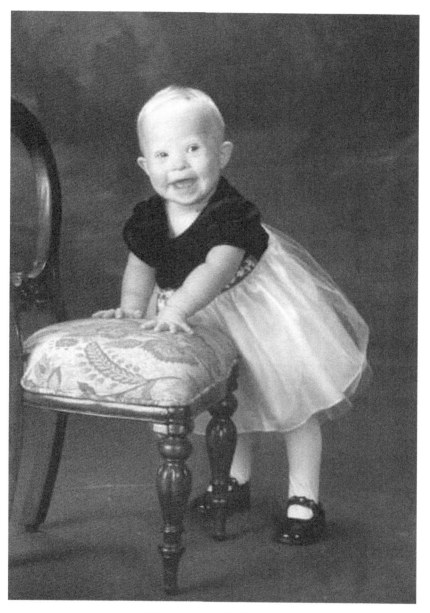

Abby at one year old, Nov 2001

Abby picking strawberries with her Papa, 2003

Abby with her younger brother Luke, June 2011

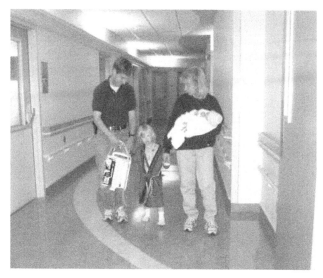

Abby's first walk after heart surgery - with Tyce, Julie, and 3-week-old Luke in March 2006

Abby and brother Luke playing in the snow, February 2011

Abby with older brother Caleb, 2002

Abby with brothers Luke and Caleb at the Fort Worth Zoo,
March 2013

Abby, October 2011

For More Information...

For more information about author Julie LaQuey and the rest of the LaQuey family, visit their website at www.laqueyfamily.com. There you will find links to books, songs, podcasts, and various other resources to help you grow in your faith. You can also contact them through their website to schedule speaking events. Be sure to inquire about their mini- conferences for churches to inspire and support parents and/or church leaders.

The LaQuey family is included in the 2022 movie titled "Kirk Cameron Presents: The Homeschool Awakening." They enjoy helping families establish firm foundations, create courage, develop delight, and live in love. Their family ministry is based on Ephesians 3:14–21. Resources on the website focus on the areas of education and homeschooling, discipleship and biblical parenting, Down syndrome and other unique needs.

You can also stay connected to the LaQuey family and their ongoing adventures through their Facebook page at LaQuey Family Adventures. Friends local to the Fort Worth area can sign up to participate in activities with other families, other moms and dads, meet with experienced parents, and receive guidance and support for biblical parenting, discipleship, and home education.

Use your phone's camera in the Spotify app to hear these songs below on Spotify!

Four Leaf Clover

Princess Lullaby

When You Feel Love From Me

Notes

1. Welcome to the Real World

1. Egan, David, and Kathleen Batato Egan. (2020) *More Alike Than Different: My Life with Down Syndrome*. Guilford: Prometheus Books.
2. Eisenberg, Arlene. (1991) *What to Expect When You're Expecting*. New York: Workman Pub.
3. Kingsley, Emily Perl. "Welcome to Holland," Accessed August 16, 2022. https://www.emilyperlkingsley.com

2. Communicate, Delegate, and Relate

1. Koch, Dr. Kathy. (2016) *8 Great Smarts*. Chicago: Moody Publishers.
2. Chapman, Gary. (2015) *The 5 Love Languages: The Secret to Love that Lasts*. Northfield Publishing.
3. Website: Focus on the Family. "4 Animals Personality Test." Accessed August 16, 2022. https://www.focusonthefamily.com/marriage/4-animals-personality-test

3. Conform or Transform: Setting and Maintaining Standards

1. Website: The Rise School. "Rise History." Accessed August 16, 2022. https://www.riseschool.org/rise-history
2. Website: Upward Sports. "Partnering with Churches to Leverage Sports in Their Community." Accessed August 16, 2022. https://www.upward.org
3. LaQuey, Julie. (2021) *Becoming Beautiful Princess Prisca*. Amazon. https://www.amazon.com/dp/B07ST4PBYB
4. Noonan, R. and Noonan, S. (2005) *The Three Weavers: Plus Companion Guide*. Pumpkin Seed Press.

4. Inward Adjustments

1. Family Life. "Weekend to Remember." Accessed August 23, 2022. https://www.familylife.com/weekend-to-remember
2. Barratt, Sara (Host). (2022, February 22). 14 Years of Doing Hard Things with Alex and Brett Harris (No. 1) [Audio podcast episode]. In Do Hard Things with

The Rebelution. Apple. https://podcasts.apple.com/us/podcast/14-years-of-doing-hard-things-with-alex-and-brett-harris/id1601060969?i=1000551865163

5. Courageous and Contagious

1. Kranowitz, C.S. & Miller, L.J. (2022) *The Out of-Sync Child: Recognizing and Coping with Sensory Processing Disorder.* TarcherPerigee, an imprint of Penguin Random House.
2. Crown. "Money Stewardship." Accessed August 20, 2022. https://www.crown.org/resource-stewardship/
3. Wilson, Durenda (Host). (2022, August 29). A Wildly Unconventional Conversation on Family Size (No. 339/351) [Audio podcast episodes]. In The Durenda Wilson Podcast. Apple. https://podcasts.apple.com/us/podcast/the-durenda-wilson-podcast/id1273544623?i=1000576580790
4. Classical Conversations. "About Classical Conversations." Accessed August 20, 2022. https://classicalconversations.com/about/
5. Kuyper, Dr. Abraham (1880, October 20) "Sphere Sovereignty." [A public address delivered at the inauguration of the Free University of Amsterdam.] Accessed September 6, 2022. https://media.thegospelcoalition.org/wp-content/uploads/2017/06/24130543/SphereSovereignty_English.pdf
6. Benge, Janet and Benge, Geoff. (1998) *Gladys Alyward: The Adventure of a Lifetime*. YWAM Publishing.

6. The End of the Matter, When All Has Been Heard: A More Accurate View of Suffering

1. Boom, T.C. (2022) *The Hiding Place*. Tyndale House Publishers.

About the Author

Julie LaQuey's titles include wife, mom, home educator, writer, musician, farm manager, and puppy wrangler. Most importantly, she loves God and strives to love others well. Julie developed her storytelling skills through years of impromptu bedtime adventures with her three children, Caleb, Abby, and Luke. She and Tyce have been married for almost 29 years.

You can join the adventure and further explore her past and ongoing stories at LaQueyFamily.com. Sign up to receive free resources and updates about future ministry activities.

35763198R00093